Jamie Russell

The Pocket Essential

VIETNAM WAR MOVIES

WITHDRAWN

First published in Great Britain 2002 by Pocket Essentials, 18 Coleswood Road, Harpenden, Herts, AL5 1EQ

Distributed in the USA by Trafalgar Square Publishing, PO Box 257, Howe Hill Road, North Pomfret, Vermont 05053

Copyright © Jamie Russell 2002
Series Editor: Steve Holland

A CIP catalogue record for this book is available from the British Library.

ISBN 1-903047-93-5

2 4 6 8 10 9 7 5 3 1

Book typeset by Wordsmith Solutions Ltd
Printed and bound by Cox & Wyman

To William,
for all his jokes about being in the 'Nam—Dagenham.

Acknowledgements

For advice, suggestions and videotapes I'd like to thank Julian Groombridge, William Groombridge, Brian Holmes, Jon and Helen Macmillan, Paul Duncan and Nev Pierce. Thanks to John and Anna Maria Groombridge for always keeping a job for me in case everything went pear shaped, to Colin and Doreen Whitehouse for all their support and interest and thanks to my mother and grandparents for always being enthusiastic about these weird projects. As always, my biggest debt is to Louise—without her this would have been impossible.

CONTENTS

1. Introduction:

"Praise The Lord And Pass The Ammunition"

All wars have a unifying theme or image that everyone recognizes. It might be a name or an event, a picture or a legend. The Battle of Hastings in 1066 is remembered because of that famous arrow in the eye, the Crimea is summed up in the Light Brigade's fatal charge, the Boer War is down in the history books as the first conflict to use concentration camps, the First World War will always be about the trenches, the Second about Hitler and the Gulf War will be remembered as a computerized, video game conflict.

The Vietnam War is unique in that the image that's most associated with the conflict is the *image* itself. It was the first—and, in many ways the last—war to be televised in all its bloody hellishness. Pictures from the battlefield were broadcast around the world in full colour by the television networks. Photographs from the conflict—like Associated Press photographer Eddie Adams' photo of the execution of a suspected Vietcong (VC) member at point blank range or the naked Vietnamese child fleeing her burning village after a napalm attack—have become ciphers for the war itself, images so famous that they're inextricably bound to the historical reality of a war that killed 58,000 Americans, left 300,000 wounded and killed 2,500,000 Vietnamese and Laotians.

As the war was transmitted into millions of American living rooms, viewers came face to face with the carnage and terror. This wasn't the carefully sanitized footage that audiences watched in cinemas during the Second World War—this was much bloodier. Families clustered around the TV to catch a glimpse of the boy from next door as he ran past the camera into a hail of bullets. Or maybe it was a son, brother or husband whose image suddenly appeared as he humped through the jungle on the other side of the world.

Unlike earlier wars, whose stories were told through memoirs, books and letters, the Vietnam conflict is dominated almost entirely by the image. Hollywood has even appropriated Vietnam writers like Michael Herr and Tim O'Brien in its quest for images of the war (Herr wrote the voiceover narration for *Apocalypse Now* and co-wrote the screenplay for *Full Metal Jacket*; O'Brien's novel *Going After Cacciato* is currently being adapted for the screen). And it's no accident that at least two comic books, Marvel's *The 'Nam* and *The Punisher* (about an ex-Marine vigilante) have emerged from the war.

Film-makers themselves have realized the importance of Vietnam as a televised event and often throw a camera crew into their battle scenes for good measure. *Full Metal Jacket* and *Apocalypse Now* both have TV newsmen filming the action (in *Apocalypse Now* it's Francis Ford Coppola himself who cameos as the TV crew's director, shouting "Don't look at the camera! Keep moving ahead, like you're fighting, like you're fighting!" at a bemused Captain Willard). In *84 Charlie Mopic* the idea is taken to its logical conclusion—a cameraman who joins a squad of infantrymen shoots the whole film. It's the ultimate statement about Vietnam and the image.

Life Through A Lens

Given the fact that the Vietnam War was dominated by images, it's hardly surprising that Hollywood steered clear of making films about the fighting in South East Asia until long after the American troops had withdrawn. Unlike the Second World War, during which propaganda films were rushed into production while the battles still raged, Vietnam was a war that no one wanted to go to the cinema to see. After all, why pay the price of a cinema ticket when you could watch the real thing in the comfort of your own home?

The Hollywood studios were canny enough to realize that Vietnam was very different from the Second World War. For all the conservatives' attempts to style the war as a just fight against a common enemy, it was difficult to motivate the American people into accepting the conflict as a 1960s version of the fight against the Nazis. After all, Vietnam was an obscure Asian backwater that few people had ever heard of until President Kennedy started shipping American military advisors and counter-insurgency troops out there in the early 1960s (and only a small minority of the American public knew that their country had been aiding the fighting in Vietnam since 1945).

The Second World War had been full of daring heroes and acts of bravery in the fight against an evil enemy. Men like Audie Murphy—America's most decorated soldier—had become heroes on the battlefields of Europe, legends in their own lifetimes. Murphy had become a celebrity after jumping onto a burning tank and mowing down a squad of advancing Germans in a selfless attempt to save his fellow soldiers. Such tales of daring were what the public wanted to see in the 1940s—so much so that Hollywood gave Murphy a contract when he came home and made him into a movie star in films like *To Hell And Back* (1955). In Vietnam, though, there were no heroes, the enemy was unseen and nobody back home wanted to know about it.

The history of Hollywood's interest in Vietnam goes back to the post-war period. Films like *Saigon* (1948), starring Alan Ladd and Veronica Lake, *The Quiet American* (1958), starring no less than Audie Murphy, and *The Ugly American* (1963), starring Marlon Brando, were politically charged dramas that tried to make blockbuster material out of the confused and confusing situation in South East Asia (to obfuscate matters more, *The Ugly American* is set in a fictional stand-in for Vietnam). Less war films than espionage dramas, these films were Hollywood's first foray into Vietnam.

The only mainstream action film to be released about America's direct involvement in the fighting was John Wayne's *The Green Berets* in 1968. At first the studios had balked at making Robin Moore's 1965 novel into a film, but John Wayne threw his clout behind the project and forced it into production since he was eager to make a significant statement about the fight against communism. The result was a one-sided, pro-war movie (the only mainstream pro-war film to come out of the Vietnam conflict) that caused uproar in the American press. Liberal critics ripped *The Green Berets* to shreds: "It is vile and insane. On top of that it is dull," claimed one critic in *The New York Times*. Wayne's militaristic fantasy about fighting the Reds was a turgid message movie and few people, apart from Wayne and a few other right-wing hawks, were willing to take its simple-minded, inaccurate and often downright ludicrous depiction of the war seriously. It didn't matter that the film was a moderate financial success (mainly as a result of the surrounding controversy in the press), Hollywood decided that Vietnam was box-office poison.

During the following ten years, the issues of Vietnam were relegated to a few low-budget exploitation pictures, the kind of cheapo productions that wouldn't be seen by enough people to register on most cultural radars (and certainly not by enough people to stir up controversy). Most of these films referenced the war in a second-hand way, dealing with veterans who'd returned from the fighting (like the 1971 *Chrome And Hot Leather* about a group of vets who take on the Hell's Angels—"Don't muck around with a green beret's mama!" warned the lurid poster) or with the attempts of young kids to avoid being shipped off to the combat zone (like the 1969 'comedy' *The Gay Deceivers*, where the two heroes pretend to be gay in order to avoid the draft).

Meanwhile, the Vietnam War played itself out. After 1969 America gradually began to withdraw its troops, a process that would lead to the 1973 ceasefire—a moment of peace that was soon broken as the North Vietnamese advanced on Saigon. The South Vietnamese capital was captured in April 1975 and as the city fell the last few Americans evacuated the Embassy in a dramatic airlift. In the meantime, America had been forced to face up to a series of catastrophes at home—the shooting of anti-war demonstrators at Kent State by National Guardsmen, the Watergate scandal and the revelations of the atrocities committed by American servicemen at My Lai. Vietnam was a cancer that seemed to have infected America from coast to coast—and Hollywood knew that no one wanted to buy tickets to see this nightmare in their local cinema.

But for all the studios' attempts to avoid the conflict, Vietnam kept creeping into the cinema—often in some very strange ways. Horror movies as diverse as *Night Of The Living Dead* (1968) and *Jaws* (1975, the year of Saigon's fall) were read as allegories of the conflict. In Romero's zombie masterpiece it's easy to interpret the 'ghouls' as 'gooks', not least of all because the policemen hunt them down in 'search and destroy' missions. Meanwhile, the Great White Shark in *Jaws* is an unstoppable killing machine (read Communism) that can only be brought to task by the efforts of a few good men (read the army) who go in and get the job done (exactly what people thought would happen in Vietnam but didn't).

Vietnam was everywhere. Non-horror films made coded references to the war in much the same way. Robert Altman's *Little Big Man* (1970) is generally regarded as the first post-Vietnam Western, a story about genocide and imperialism that had as much to do with South East Asia as it did with Native Americans. In other films, screen violence itself seemed to be echoing the carnage that was taking place overseas, with *Bonnie And Clyde* (1967) and *The Wild Bunch* (1969) competing against the televised pictures from the combat zone in terms of blood and guts. *M*A*S*H* (1969) may have been ostensibly set in Korea, but everyone knew it was really about Vietnam. *Deliverance* (1972) may have been set in America's forests, but that didn't fool anyone into thinking it wasn't about the war. Even seemingly innocuous films like Martin Scorsese's six-minute short "The Big Shave" (1967)—in which a man continues shaving for so long that the razor rips the bloody skin off his cheeks—seemed to be influenced by Vietnam (the relentless shave and the blood-filled sink are a potential metaphor for America's masochistic involvement in South East Asia).

Years after the war, Vietnam remained a spectral presence in Hollywood's nightmares. Consider *Southern Comfort* (1981). An action set in the swamps of the Deep South or an echo of the guerrilla warfare of Vietnam? What about *Aliens* (1986) and *Predator* (1987)? Science fiction films or allegories of Vietnam in which colonial space marines and Special Forces units find their tactical and military superiority overcome by (biologically) primitive 'aliens'?

Putting The War On Film

1978 was the year that Hollywood finally felt ready to face up to Vietnam, with four major studio releases hitting cinemas in rapid succession: *The Boys In Company C*, *Coming Home*, *The Deer Hunter*, and *Go Tell The Spartans*. Then in 1979, delayed because of logistical problems during filming (an understatement if ever there was one), came the release of *Apocalypse Now*, Francis Ford Coppola's epic absurdist masterpiece.

Cinema audiences were suddenly bombarded with Hollywood product specifically about the Vietnam War and it was these five films that laid down the main subgenres: the combat film (*Go Tell The Spartans* and *The Boys In Company C*), the anti-war protest film (*Coming Home*), the vet film (*The Deer Hunter*), and the drug-addled, surreal 'Nam movie (*Apocalypse Now*). In the years that followed, Hollywood's willingness to face up to the war also brought two more subgenres: the mid-1980s *Rambo*-cycle of comic strip action films and the series of left-field approaches to the conflict that emerged in the late 1980s and early 1990s that dealt with the war from different perspectives (of course, very few of these apart from *Heaven & Earth* were Hollywood productions).

But why was 1978 the year that America suddenly felt it could cope with seeing Vietnam on the screen? Partly it was the inevitable force of history. As time passed and old wounds healed, Vietnam became a more acceptable topic of conversation. But, more interestingly, economic factors also played an important role. The modest success of low-budget exploitation films that tapped into the Vietnam story convinced the major studios that there was money to be made in packaging the war for cinema audiences. The Billy Jack series—*The Born Losers* (1967), *Billy Jack* (1971), *The Trial of Billy Jack* (1974) and *Billy Jack Goes To Washington* (1977)—told the story of a Vietnam veteran who returns home to fight rednecks and Hell's Angels. It proved such a money-spinning success that several studios kicked themselves for not coming up with the formula first.

Although the Billy Jack series took place in America, its use of a Vietnam veteran as a vigilante superhero suggested to the studio executives that the war wasn't necessarily a taboo subject. If audiences went wild for Billy Jack's blend of action, 'Nam veterans and good ol' boy fist fights, then perhaps a war film set in Vietnam wasn't such an outlandish idea.

Making Sense Of It All

The history of Vietnam War films isn't a history of the war itself. Watching films from *Go Tell The Spartans* to *The Deer Hunter*, *First Blood* or *Platoon* won't give you much idea about the realities of the war in Vietnam. Sure you'll learn about the experiences of the grunts in the field, or the treatment of veterans once they returned home, but you'd be unlikely to answer any questions about the history of the war in South East Asia. Films about the Second World War give audiences the chance to learn a little about the history of the conflict—there are stories about the D-Day landings and the fighting in Europe (*The Longest Day*), historic events (*The Dambusters*), the desert campaigns (*The Desert Fox*) and the Pacific theatre (*Hell In The Pacific*). Watch enough films about the Second World War and you'll get a sense of the historical events that shaped the battles.

Surprisingly, Vietnam War films can't match this sense of historical perspective. Aside from several recreations of the Tet Offensive, or a few veiled allusions to the My Lai massacre, most of the films aren't set around the momentous events of the time—there's no film that even mentions the contentious Gulf of Tonkin incident that brought America into the war. In fact, all but a handful of the films set 'in country' occur either in the moments before or in the aftermath of the Tet Offensive of 1968 when the North Vietnamese took America by surprise and turned the tide of the war in their favour. And the only reason why the Tet Offensive is such a popular subject is because it was the one battle of the war that—as the bloody carnage of *Platoon*'s recreation of it illustrates—was ripe for being made into blockbuster material.

Part of the reason why Vietnam War films seem so historically lost is because of the nature of the war itself. Most films focus on the realities of the day-to-day fighting 'in country', battles that took place in dense jungles against an enemy that frequently couldn't be seen. As historians so often tell us, Vietnam was a war of brief skirmishes, a guerrilla war that American troops weren't prepared to cope with (more than one historian has suggested that if Nixon had ordered a conventional sea-land invasion of North Vietnam, capturing the capital Ho Chi Minh city, the war could well have been winnable). There wasn't any 'home ground', there was no sense of winning or losing—just kill ratios and casualty figures. In the light of all this, it's not surprising that Vietnam War films never give much of an overview of the conflict.

But there's a more important reason for this lack of historical perspective. While Second World War films are largely about celebrating victory, Vietnam War films are about trying to make sense of a catastrophic and completely unexpected defeat. The history of Vietnam War films is a history of American responses to the war, of the American public's desire for closure and for the healing of old wounds. They're not films about a war, but about an American tragedy. No one's particularly interested in the history of the war—after all, history belongs to victors. Rather, what's at stake is a process of trying to heal the nation's injuries. As Francis Ford Coppola commented on *Apocalypse Now*, his aim was "cauterising old wounds, trying to let people put the war behind them. You can never do that by forgetting it."

The history of Vietnam War films from 1978 to the present is closely tied to this aim. After the 1978-1979 establishment of Vietnam as a suitable subject for blockbuster treatment, the genre became an acceptable vehicle for directors and scriptwriters. But this new-found interest in the war didn't maintain its integrity for long. By the early 1980s, the war films had become cardboard vehicles for a reactionary conservatism that, spearheaded by President Ronald Reagan, was sweeping the nation. After the brief popularity of respectable war films like *Coming Home*, *Go Tell The Spartans* or *Apocalypse Now*, Hollywood returned to the cheap, exploitative output that had characterized the late 1960s and early 1970s (the veterans films) only this time in combat and with a transparent right-wing ideology.

The 'Return to 'Nam' subgenre began with *Uncommon Valor* in 1983 and proceeded (with the help of Sylvester Stallone and Chuck Norris) to make Vietnam War films into facile comic book fantasies about re-fighting the war, getting the gooks and generally proving once and for all that America didn't deserve to lose Saigon. This was a cinema of vengeance, a re-match that had redneck audiences cheering every time John Rambo opened fire with his M-60.

The 'Return to 'Nam' cycle didn't last very long. In fact, it actually inspired another group of film-makers to seize the moment and revitalize the serious war films of the late 1970s. From around 1986, Vietnam escaped *Rambo*-ization and was back at the Oscars. Oliver Stone's *Platoon*, followed by John Irvin's *Hamburger Hill* and Stanley Kubrick's *Full Metal Jacket* reinvented the genre. Much was made of the fact that unlike the films of the late 1970s, these three productions featured prominent contributions from men who had actually fought in the war

14

itself. In comparison with film school graduates such as Coppola, both Irvin and Stone had had first-hand experience of the front line—Irvin as a documentary film-maker and Stone as a grunt. Indeed, the hype surrounding *Platoon* made much out of the fact that Stone was a "decorated infantryman who had spent fifteen months" 'in country' (Stanley Kubrick couldn't claim the same credentials, but *Full Metal Jacket* did follow this pattern of fictionalizing the war from the point of view of those involved—the film was based on a novel by an infantryman and was adapted with the help of war correspondent Michael Herr).

Authenticity was the new buzzword, and these three films wore their "I was there" credentials on their cinematic sleeves (the documentary *Dear America: Letters Home From Vietnam*, based on the letters of real soldiers, was also part of this sudden resurgence of interest in authenticity). The *Bildungsroman* format of *Platoon* and *Full Metal Jacket* stressed the importance of the grunt's individual point of view (Privates Chris and Joker). Stuck "in the shit," they had little idea of the big picture, but could comment on the realities of jungle warfare against the VC and North Vietnamese Army. By focussing on the minutiae of combat experience—in *Hamburger Hill* one character complains about the long, long list of things that have to be remembered in order to survive—all three of these films tried to put the 'truth' of the day-to-day realities of warfare on the screen.

But, it wasn't as easy as the film-makers hoped. As so many critics have pointed out, by focussing on the individual and the specific, Hollywood's second wave of Vietnam War films only ended up obscuring the bigger picture. Where were the scenes of anti-war protestors back home? Why did we never learn anything about the VC (except how ruthless they were supposed to be)? Why were we never told what objectives these men were fighting for? Trying to make sense of the war—Hollywood style—only reduced the conflict to a few choice facts and left out any that didn't fit into the pattern of a combat movie (what, for instance, should we make of the fact that no mainstream American combat film shows any of the thousands of female American service personnel who were present in Vietnam?).

It's a sad fact about the Vietnam War genre that films that aren't obsessed with combat can never compete against the grunt movies, the

'Return to 'Nam' films or the action blockbusters. Films about the protest movement—like *Vietnam Day Berkeley: 1965* (1965), *No Vietnamese Ever Called Me Nigger* (1968, the title comes from Mohammad Ali's famous justification for not fighting in the "white man's war"), or *Kent State* (1981)—have been rendered invisible because they can't compete against the action spectaculars for domination of the public's attention.

Even the most liberal anti-war sentiments, like those expressed in *Platoon*, take on a slightly different feel when they occur in a combat movie. Can any film that relies on action, shooting and dead bodies to grip the audience's attention really be anti-war? Isn't an anti-war combat film something of an oxymoron? Watching *Platoon* you certainly realize that war is hell—but this feeling has to compete with the more immediate adrenalin rush of the battle scenes that, for all their visceral horror, are always exciting.

In the 1990s, Oliver Stone tried to redress the balance with two films—*Born On The Fourth Of July* and *Heaven & Earth*—that sought to get away from the battlefield and tell a different story about the war, from the perspective of the counter-culture and from that of a Vietnamese woman respectively. It was a commendable effort, but one that couldn't make up for the fact that the bulk of films about the Vietnam War that are widely seen are combat movies.

In researching this book the extent of Hollywood's domination of the war became apparent. Finding films like *The Activist* (1969) or *Fairy Tale For Seventeen Year Olds* (*Truyen Co Tich Cho Tuoi 17*, 1987) is near impossible. They've either never had a video release or have been deleted. Most can't be found in even the most comprehensive video catalogues. They've been completely silenced. It's a sad fact that most Americans' understanding of the 1960s protestors is likely to be informed by the revisionist *Forrest Gump*.

The Eastern Western

If most Hollywood Vietnam War films are about trying to make sense of the war, trying to understand what happened and why, then it's fair to say that the most often used shorthand for trying to put the war

16

into perspective is the Western. Vietnam War films are obsessed with the Western genre for obvious reasons. The Western is, after all, a story about America's identity as a nation, an identity that the defeat in South East Asia thoroughly undermined.

From *The Green Berets* to *The Deer Hunter* and *Full Metal Jacket*, the Western has always been an integral part of the combat film. It also appears in vet movies like *First Blood* and even druggy movies like *Apocalypse Now*. From the moment that John Wayne rode into 'Fort Dodge' on the back of a Huey, the Western became the template that all combat films would use to some extent or another.

After all, the Western was a battle that Americans knew by heart. It was the white man facing the dark-skinned savage; the movement of progress and civilization against primitivism (in *Gardens Of Stone* one character incredulously mentions reports that the VC are attacking helicopters with arrows); the frontier spirit that underpinned the American Dream. Only this time it wasn't a movement West, but East, into the heart of communism's darkness.

Building a civilization out in the wilderness validated the use of violence. After all, violence was how the West was won. What's more, like the good guys in so many Hollywood Westerns, the American troops were helping the South Vietnamese—the frightened townsfolk/settlers of a hundred and one Westerns who couldn't live peacefully without being attacked by the Indians (or Communists). The American army became a latter day version of John Wayne's cavalry soldiers from *Fort Apache*.

In the hands of skilful directors like Michael Cimino these Western elements became more than just a set of clichés. In *The Deer Hunter*, Cimino turns the Western theme (with Michael as a contemporary forest ranger) into a telling window on America's mythic self-identity. After all, as we'll see, Vietnam War films aren't about the war but about America's attempts to get over defeat and redefine what 'America' actually represents.

2. "Hard Core, Man":

The Vietnam Combat Movie

In the Second World War the average age of the combat soldier was twenty-six. In Vietnam he was—as anyone who was around in 1985 when Paul Hardcastle's song hit the top ten will remember—just nineteen. Volunteers and then draftees were shipped out into the combat zone and confronted with a war that had been raging for decades before they were born. It was a baptism of fire that would leave 58,000 of them dead.

Hollywood's treatment of the war in the post-Vietnam era was vastly different from the heroic action of the combat films that came out of the Second World War. While the earliest Vietnam combat movies (*Go Tell The Spartans* and *The Boys In Company C*) often used the Second World War platoon movie as a starting point, they always went on to show that the war in South East Asia was completely different from the fight against Nazism. All preconceived ideas about heroism and just causes are cynically dismissed in both *Go Tell The Spartans* and *The Boys In Company C*. There are no heroes, only idiots and cannon fodder. The ending of *Go Tell The Spartans* sums up the overriding feeling of both movies—it was a dumb war and America was even dumber for getting sucked into it. There's no place here for honour, heroism or self-sacrifice and even an iconic actor like Burt Lancaster, the star of so many Second World War films, gets shot to pieces—significantly, his final words are devoid of all heroism. All he manages to whisper is "Oh shit!"

With the exception of *The Green Berets* and the later 'Return to 'Nam' films of the early 1980s, most Hollywood visions of the war were always keen to play up the negative aspects of the conflict. Perhaps that's why the combat film suffered such a hiatus between 1978 and 1986. Everyone already knew that the war was dumb and that Vietnam was hell—they didn't need a bunch of know-nothing Hollywood types to tell them that. But by 1986, as the post-Vietnam generation hit the multiplexes, there was room for a new kind of combat film, one told by men who'd been there and seen the battles with their own eyes. *Platoon*, *Hamburger Hill* and *Full Metal Jacket* made the Vietnam War film respectable again. Imitators like *Casualties Of War* built upon their success (but couldn't quite copy the formula) and as recent entries like *Tigerland* prove, the war may be long finished, but it's still a good excuse for an action movie.

In comparison with films about the Vietnam War, the combat film has always needed the big-budget pyrotechnics that only a bankable director can secure. As a result, the scope of the combat film has always been somewhat limited. While low-budget independent and exploitation directors were able to experiment with stories of returning veterans (which didn't need any expensive special effects or battlefield sequences), the combat genre has always been the preserve of those directors with at least some studio clout. Perhaps if John Milius and George Lucas had carried out their original plan to shoot *Apocalypse Now* in 16mm on the battlefields of Vietnam while the war was raging, a different breed of combat films might have been established. But sadly that exciting idea became a $30 million studio picture.

The Green Berets (1968)

Crew: Director: John Wayne, Ray Kellogg. Producer: Michael Wayne. Writer: James Lee Barrett, from the novel *The Green Berets* by Robin Moore. Cinematographer: Winton C Hoch. Editor: Otho Lovering.

Cast: John Wayne (Colonel Mike Kirby), David Janssen (George Beckworth), Jim Hutton (Sergeant Petersen), Aldo Ray (Sergeant Muldoon), Raymond St Jacques (Doc McGee).

Summary: Green Beret Colonel Mike Kirby takes a squad out to Vietnam. Reinforcing a camp on the Laos/Cambodia border, Kirby and his men fend off VC attacks but finally have to retreat and call in an air strike. After securing the camp again, Kirby leads a mission to capture an important VC officer using a South Vietnamese woman as bait. The mission is successful, but the human cost in terms of lives lost is high.

Subtext: The only pro-war film to have ever been produced about the Vietnam War, *The Green Berets* is a facile piece of jingoistic, macho propaganda that even the hawks felt compelled to dismiss because it was too inaccurate and so laughably blinkered to the realities of war in Vietnam. While many Vietnam War films reference the Western, John Wayne's *The Green Berets* has the distinction of being the only film that believes it is a cowboys and indians fight!

Background: The Green Berets was a project that John Wayne spent a huge amount of time and money trying to get off the ground. Although the studios were against making the film—fearing, quite rightly, that the ongoing war was too emotive to be used as a source of cinema entertainment—Wayne used all his Hollywood clout to force the script into production, even securing the Pentagon's help with military vehicles, sets and technical advice. In preparation for his role he toured South Vietnam, meeting the troops and signing autographs (not to mention, as legend has it, coming under sniper fire).

The result of the Duke's enthusiastic energies is a movie that is both technically inept (one of the most famous gaffes is the final sunset, where the sun sets in the East—quite inappropriately for the South China sea) and politically offensive. Imagining the Vietnam War in terms of the Western, *The Green Berets* pits the whites against the yellow Indians. Apart from a handful of stereotypically 'good' Vietnamese (loyal, noble savages one and all), the majority of the film's Asians are never characterized as anything other than primitive peasants, whose unsporting tactics include pit traps and sharpened spears daubed with excrement.

The Western echoes reach a crescendo as Wayne's character, named Colonel Kirby after Wayne's hero in John Ford's cavalry films *Fort Apache* and *Rio Grande*, rides into Vietnam on the back of his helicopter and sets up camp in the appropriately nicknamed 'Fort Dodge' When the VC storm the camp, looting the bodies of the dead, the soundtrack hammers home the parallels by dredging up the kind of stereotypical Native American music last heard in the Westerns of the 1930s and 1940s. No wonder liberal critics were incensed when the film was first released.

That *The Green Berets* is a message movie is made perfectly clear in the opening sequences, where a handful of soldiers explain the dangers of international communism to a group of civilians at Fort Bragg. The

20

American journalist who accompanies the squad to Vietnam transforms during the course of the film from hand-wringing liberal wimp to rugged, combat experienced pro-war supporter as he realizes—thanks to the Duke's clarification—that the VC aren't freedom fighter but ruthless murderers backed by the Reds. What is at stake isn't some corner of a foreign field, but instead the fight against the "communist domination of the world." The film's rather blatant aim is to brainwash the audience into undergoing Beckworth's conversion to the good fight against the commies.

The Boys In Company C (1978)

Crew: Director: Sidney Furie. Producer: Andrew Morgan. Writer: Rick Natkin. Cinematographer: Godfrey Godfar. Editors: Michael Berman, Frank T Urioste, Alan Patillo, James Benson.

Cast: Stan Shaw (Tyrone Washington), Michael Lembeck (Vinnie Fazio), James Canning (Alvin Foster), Craig Wasson (Dave Bisbee).

Summary: A group of American army recruits are put through basic training by their drill instructor at Fort Bragg. Arriving in Vietnam, they discover that the war is not as clear cut as they previously believed— instead of a simple good vs. evil fight they find a situation in which America's role isn't easily justified. The chain of command is bureaucratic and incompetent, the South Vietnamese allies are brutal and corrupt and American boys are even asked to lose a football game against the South Vietnamese regulars (or be sent into the heart of the action). Naturally the troops aren't keen on the idea and end up marching off into battle and certain death.

Subtext: War is hell—the world is corrupt—and there's not a damn thing anyone can do about it.

Background: Directed by Sidney Furie, *The Boys In Company C* is a particularly bleak addition to the 1978 wave of Vietnam films. Its unerringly nihilistic viewpoint is no doubt the reason why it fared so poorly at the late-1970s box office and has subsequently sunk into obscurity. At first glance, the film appears to be a conventional war story, with the old boot camp/combat zone formula that would later be used in films like *Full Metal Jacket* and *Tigerland*. However, *The Boys In Company*

C's temperament is quite unlike any other Vietnam film—it's so darkly pessimistic that it throws the whole conflict into disrepute and points an accusatory finger at America for letting the war take so many lives. The ragtag platoon of soldiers—clichéd characters that include a wannabe writer, a drug dealer and the inevitable hippie—is placed in the same position as the men of *Go Tell The Spartans*. The war is being so atrociously mismanaged and none of the lessons they learned in boot camp (where Lee Ermey drills them in a slightly less profane version of his similar role in *Full Metal Jacket*) can save them from the fact that the war is unwinnable and ultimately futile. In the tradition of *Go Tell The Spartans*, *Apocalypse Now* and *Good Morning Vietnam*, *The Boys In Company C* believes that the war isn't just hell it's totally absurd—as pointlessly stupid as being asked to throw a soccer match to one's allies.

Go Tell The Spartans (1978)

Crew: Director: Ted Post. Producer: Allan F Bodah, Mitchell Cannoed. Writer: Wendell Mayes, based on the novel *Incident At Muc Wa* by Daniel Ford. Cinematographer: Henry Stradling Jnr. Editor: Millie Moore.

Cast: Burt Lancaster (Major Barker), Craig Wasson (Corporal Courcey), Jonathan Goldsmith (Sergeant Oleonowski), Marc Singer (Captain Olivetti).

Summary: Vietnam, 1964. Major Barker is in charge of a group of Military Advisory Command officers who are aiding the South Vietnamese Army. Ordered to garrison a deserted hamlet called Muc Wa, Barker sends out a ragtag group of American soldiers and Vietnamese fighters under the command of an inexperienced new Lieutenant. The VC attack the compound and the Lieutenant is killed in an act of foolish heroism. The camp is left in the command of Corporal Courcey. As the Americans realize that the hamlet has no strategic importance, Major Baxter arrives to fly the troops out, but there's not enough room in the helicopter for the Vietnamese fighters. Corporal Courcey refuses to leave them behind and so he stays with Major Barker to try and lead their retreat. Everyone's killed when the VC attack except for the Corporal, who is so disillusioned with the war he wants to return home.

Subtext: Go Tell The Spartans presents the war as an insane undertaking. Building on the absurd vision of *M*A*S*H* and prefiguring the madness of *Apocalypse Now*, *Go Tell The Spartans* is full of ridiculous incidents: the new lieutenant is sent on "mosquito patrol" to count how many bugs land on his exposed arms in thirty seconds; the cynical Major Barker invents reconnaissance reports because he's understaffed while complaining "sometimes I get the feeling we're in a goddamned loony bin" and vital air support is only granted after a series of violent threats are sent up the chain of command.

Background. Go Tell The Spartans is unusual in that it is one of the few films to deal with America's advisory role in Vietnam during the early 1960s. Released in 1978, along with *The Boys In Company C*, *The Deer Hunter* and *Coming Home*, Ted Post's film is a nihilistic, cynical and decidedly anti-heroic addition to the combat film subgenre. It wears its anti-war sentiments on its sleeve, relying on Burt Lancaster's haggard visage to symbolize the difference between Vietnam and earlier wars; Lancaster is, after all, an actor more often associated with decidedly more heroic Westerns and Second World War films. Major Baxter knows that the Vietnam conflict is pointless, yet he also believes that America has a moral duty to help the Vietnamese—the problem is that between the corruption in South Vietnam and the incompetence of the American military, there's little hope of the outcome being successful. As *Go Tell The Spartans* makes painfully clear, this is a war that the French already lost in 1954, a war that in 1964 had become America's problem but was still "confused and far away." The title—a classical reference that is written above the graveyard containing French soldiers—suggests that following stupid orders often leads to death. The rest of the Vietnam conflict after 1964 was to prove that rule time and time again.

Platoon (1986)

Crew: Director: Oliver Stone. Producer: Arnold Kopelson. Writer: Oliver Stone. Cinematographer: Robert Richardson. Editor: Claire Simpson.

Cast: Tom Berenger (Sergeant Barnes) Willem Dafoe (Sergeant Elias) Charlie Sheen (Private Chris Taylor), Forrest Whitaker (Big Harold), Francesco Quinn (Rhah Ramucci).

Summary: Taylor, a 19-year-old infantry soldier, is shipped out to Vietnam. The platoon he joins is split between Sergeants Barnes and Elias. After a Vietnamese village is torched and several villagers are unlawfully killed (by Barnes), the tensions in the group worsen. Barnes kills Elias. The Tet Offensive begins and the platoon is decimated in a night of fighting. Taylor is injured and finally gets shipped back home.

Subtext: Resolutely sticking to the grunt's story, *Platoon* is Oliver Stone's semi-autobiographical story based on his own experiences as an infantryman. As Taylor realizes at the end of the film, Barnes and Elias represent two sides of personality (good and evil, perhaps) that are fighting for "possession of my soul." As long as the war continues the grunts will have to measure their actions in these terms.

Background: Oliver Stone's startling multi-Oscar winning drama is probably the best-known, most highly admired film to have emerged from the Vietnam conflict. In comparison with such monstrous works as *Apocalypse Now*, *Platoon* is a relatively modest film that tries to show audiences the realities of the fighting in Vietnam. When it was released in 1986, the film became the centre of a storm of controversy, as old, unhealed wounds were reopened. Many vets hailed the film as the first truthful telling of the war, while others dismissed it as inaccurate. The film's reworking of the My Lai massacre was destined particularly to raise heckles. After the simple wish-fulfilment ideology of the reactionary *Rambo* cycle, Stone re-politicized the Vietnam War film making it, once again, the vehicle for serious comment on the nature of the South East Asia conflict rather than the hiding place of big muscles and small brains.

Yet, having said all that, *Platoon* is still somewhat simplistic. The obvious dichotomy of Elias and Barnes and their squads is pretty black and white (the good guys vs. the bad guys; the doves vs. the hawks; the stoners vs. the rednecks). Elias' near-messianic posture (Barnes claims he's a "water-walker") and his carefully constructed death scene set to the mournful strains of Barber's *Adagio for Strings*, mark him out as a martyred saint, while Barnes' scarred face and mean, redneck attitude are clearly meant to make him seem demonic. Not even Sheen's voice-over (an echo of his father's narration in *Apocalypse Now*) can add much depth to the proceedings, leaving *Platoon* caught somewhere between an exciting, bloody combat film and a liberal "war is hell" vehicle. Or, in other words, caught between Barnes and Elias. But, in refocusing the Vietnam War film genre on the grass roots of the grunts' experiences, *Platoon* revitalized the combat film by mixing action with political commitment in a way that its imitators, especially *Hamburger Hill* and *Full Metal Jacket*, never quite managed to copy.

Hamburger Hill (1987)

Crew: Director: John Irvin. Producers: Marcia Nasatir, James Carabatsos. Writer: James Carabatsos. Cinematographer: Peter MacDonald. Editor: Peter Tanner.

Cast: Dylan McDermott (Frantz), Steven Weber (Worcester), Tim Quill (Beletsky), Don Cheadle (Washburn), Michael Patrick Boatman (Motown).

Summary: As the Americans renew their attack on the Ashau valley in May 1969, a squad of the 101st Airborne receive a group of rookie replacements and are sent back into the fighting. Having already lost a lot of men in the region, the old-timers in the squad are unhappy about being saddled with "cherries." After some R&R the attack on Hill 937 begins and the troops encounter fierce resistance. The squad is depleted one by one until only three of the original group remain.

Subtext: Hamburger Hill is a film about names, naming and anonymity. It opens with a blurry shot of the Vietnam memorial in Washington, as the camera skims over the names of the fallen. The fact that the shot is slightly out of focus means that none of the names are legible—these are the anonymous casualties of war.

The action of the film follows much the same approach. Everyone's obsessed with names, from the sergeant who already knows "too many names" of fallen comrades, to the Italian-American soldier who's called "Alphabet" because no one can pronounce his surname and the medic who can't identify a dead soldier whose head (and dog tags) has been blown off. Even the hill that the film takes place on is an anonymous lump of mud—known only as Hill 937 and no different from any of the · other hundreds of hills in the Ashau valley.

The casting continues the theme. These actors are complete unknowns (only Don Cheadle would go on to become famous) and as they're picked off one after the other it's often difficult to distinguish who's who. War, it would seem, really is anonymous.

Background: Hot on the heels of *Platoon*, *Hamburger Hill* follows the post-1985 trend for realistic combat films that take a grunt's point of view. Rather than give an overview of the war, *Hamburger Hill* is firmly rooted in the personal, following a handful of men as they fight their way up the slopes of Hill 937. It's certainly one of the dirtiest Vietnam War films, imagining the battle as a giant mudslide in which blood and guts mix with rain and soil. This emphasis on grim reality ties the film to its Korean War counterpart, Lewis Milestone's *Pork Chop Hill* (1959). But whereas Gregory Peck gave a rousing speech in the finale of that film about the importance of the battle in terms of world freedom (a speech that was apparently tacked on by the studios without Milestone's consent), *Hamburger Hill* valiantly resists any heroic interpretation—this is war as a bloody, pointless hell on earth.

Full Metal Jacket (1987)

Crew: Director: Stanley Kubrick. Producer: Stanley Kubrick. Writers: Stanley Kubrick, Michael Herr, Gustav Hasford, based on the novel *The Short-Timers* by Gustav Hasford. Cinematographer: Douglas Milsome. Editor: Martin Hunter.

Cast: Matthew Modine (Private 'Joker'), Adam Baldwin (Animal Mother), Vincent D'Onofrio (Private 'Pyle'), Lee Ermey (Gunnery Sergeant Hartman), Arliss Howard (Private 'Cowboy').

Summary: Parris Island marine training centre. A group of new recruits arrive and are put under the charge of the aggressive drill instructor. Moulding them into fighting men the instructor takes exception to a fat recruit nicknamed 'Pyle' and targets him for abuse. At the end of the training Pyle loses the plot and kills the instructor and then himself. Vietnam, 1968. Journalist Private Joker is shipped out to cover the fighting of the Tet Offensive. The unit he joins comes under attack from a female sniper. Joker finds the sniper and kills her.

Subtext: Full Metal Jacket's two distinct segments focus on the dehumanising processes of military training and combat experience to suggest that the processes of warfare are ones in which individualism is always the first casualty.

Background: Dehumanization was always one of Stanley Kubrick's grand themes. From *2001: A Space Odyssey* to *A Clockwork Orange*, it was a concern that he repeatedly returned to. The opening thirty minutes of *Full Metal Jacket* takes the theme to new levels. From the moment that Lee Ermey's drill instructor opens his mouth, his is the voice that dominates—the audience and the recruits are subjected to his anxiety-inducing barrage of abuse (Ermey, a real-life drill instructor and ex-marine from Vietnam, whose film career as an advisor and actor spans *The Boys In Company C*, *Apocalypse Now* and *Purple Hearts*, told Kubrick that most films about boot camp "have too much gabbing" in them).

Taking Ermey's comments as a starting point, the screenplay of *Full Metal Jacket*, written with the help of Michael Herr *(Dispatches)*, focuses on the ways in which the marines' training depersonalises and dehumanises each individual recruit in order to create group cohesion. The tormenting of Private Pyle, begun at the drill instructor's behest, is designed to strengthen the rest of the group. Yet, there's also a more important dynamic occurring. Kubrick's film pivots on the opposition of the masculine and the feminine. Pyle, whose fat body and inept behaviour obviously mark him out as 'feminized', is expelled from the group because he is not 'hard' or 'masculine' enough. Ermey's profanities repeatedly encourage the recruits to transform themselves from 'ladies' to *real* men by becoming 'hardcore'.

The second section of the film, in which Joker and the squad encounter a female sniper (her gender is no mere accident), builds on the opening's thematic opposition of the individual/the group and masculine/feminine. Joker (the cynical marine who's opted to work as an army journalist instead of fighting as an infantryman) finally puts his marine training into practice, becoming truly 'hardcore' as he ruthlessly executes the female sniper. With one shot he's able to prove his macho credentials to the rest of the platoon and finally expel the feminine once and for all.

BAT*21 (1988)

Crew: Director: Peter Markle. Producers: David Fisher, Gary A Neill, Michael Balson. Writer: William C Anderson, George Gordon, based on the book by William C Anderson. Cinematographer: Marc Irwin. Editor: Stephen E Rivkin.

Cast: Gene Hackman (Lt. Colonel Hambleton), Danny Glover (Captain Clark), Jerry Reed (Colonel Walker), Grant Marshall (Ross Carver).

Summary: When army reconnaissance expert Lt. Col. Hambleton is shot down over Vietnam a rescue operation is mounted to keep him from falling into enemy hands. Hambleton's knowledge of a forthcoming bombing mission makes him a valuable prize to the VC. Spotter plane pilot Captain 'Birdog' Clark keeps the grounded officer company from the air as he dodges the VC and tries to escape the area before the raid commences. But Hambleton finds that war on the ground is a lot more personal than from 30,000 feet above the battlefield.

Subtext: The oldies are the goodies. Aging fly boys Hambleton and Clark are the sensible, caring sensitive face of modern warfare. Hotshot young pilots like Carver treat the war as a game and end up suffering the consequences.

Background: A late entry in the 1980s search for authenticity, Bat*21 is both part of and a reaction against the Platoon cycle of films. Like Platoon and its imitators, Bat*21 relies on a real-life combat veteran for input. The true story of Hambleton's crash as told in William C Anderson's book offers something more 'real' than the *Rambo* fantasies of the mid-1980s. But, unlike Platoon, Hamburger Hill and Full Metal Jacket, Bat*21 isn't interested in young grunts but in aging air force pilots. Youth, according to the film, is a curse and the war would clearly be better off being left to more sensible aging warriors like Hackman and Glover. The young pilot who ignores orders and tries to land in a hot LZ to save Hambleton is killed along with his crew. Meanwhile, on the ground, Hambleton realizes that gung-ho heroics are meaningless. He gets to see the real consequences of his actions—the dead civilians, VC soldiers and bombed-out countryside that America's technological superiority is producing. Losing faith in the war, Hackman and Glover's characters have a crisis of conscience. The war is clearly wrong on a humanitarian level. Hambleton's comment that "It's probably time to find another way of making a living" isn't quite as flippant as it might sound. This Lt. Colonel has realized that the war is being mismanaged and has to face up to the fact that it's men like him who are responsible for so many deaths. As he calls in air strikes from ground level, he gets to see 'up close and personal' the effect that his bombing raids actually have. "People keep dying all around me," he complains, finally realizing that there's more to Vietnam than the golf fairways that he's first seen playing on.

Saigon (aka Off Limits) (1988)

Crew: Director: Christopher Crowe. Producer: Alan Barnette. Writers: Christopher Crowe, Jack Thibeau. Cinematographer: David Gribble. Editor: Doug Ibold.

Cast: Willem Dafoe (Buck McGriff), Gregory Hines (Albaby Perkins), Fred Ward (Sergeant Dix), Amanda Pays (Nicole).

Summary: US Army cops Buck and Albaby are assigned to investigate a series of prostitute murders in pre-Tet Saigon. The evidence points to a high-ranking US Army officer and the cops find that their superiors are blocking the investigation at every turn. With the help of local French nun Nicole, the cops narrow down their list of suspects to just two men. But could they have overlooked something?

Subtext: Saigon is the "cess pool of the world," a beacon of moral, spiritual and political corruption on a par with Sodom and Gomorrah.

The South Vietnamese are VC sympathizers, whores or villains and as such don't deserve to have American boys dying for their freedom. What's worse, the immorality of Saigon is also corrupting stand-up American soldiers, perverting them into killers and sadists.

Background: Misogynist, racist and deeply disturbing, *Saigon* is an unusual entry in the Vietnam War cycle. By all accounts it ought to be a vet movie (with a white/black buddy partnership that recalls everything from *The Exterminator* to *Lethal Weapon*). But it's actually set in Saigon during the war with two scenes set 'in country', one during the Tet Offensive and the other on a helicopter where a cracked Colonel (played by Scott Glen) is interrogating and 'body-bombing' VC suspects. While it would be easier to dismiss *Saigon* as just a formulaic 1980s thriller that uses Vietnam as an exotic backdrop, the film's politics are actually in keeping with those of the combat film.

The film ostensibly sets itself up as yet another Western with the two heroes—"a pair of Gary Coopers"—trying to clean up the lawless city of Saigon ("civilians, troops, gangsters, cowboys, deserters, dopers, black marketeers—God I love this town!"). But as the story unfolds, the script's racist and misogynist elements come to dominate. The "slopes, gooks and slant-eyed VC motherfuckers" bear the brunt of the film's displeasure as Dafoe's and Hines' characters gleefully torment, beat and generally abuse any South Vietnamese they get their hands on while maintaining a running battle with the local 'white mice'.

Tellingly, women are styled as either white-skinned angels or yellow-skinned whores—quite literally since the only female characters are Asian prostitutes and a French Catholic nun (!). As the killer reveals his identity, the extent of the film's distrust of the feminine becomes apparent. Women are only good for one thing (or, if you're a psychotic killer, two things) and pleasure (symbolized by Saigon itself) needs to be policed so that it doesn't make men lose control (become feminized). The film ends with Nicole being confirmed as a nun while the two leads joke about a local prostitute who has the biggest nipples ever seen. So much for feminism, then.

84 Charlie Mopic (1989)

Crew: Director: Patrick Duncan. Producers: Michael Nolin, Jill Griffith. Writer: Patrick Duncan. Cinematographer: Alan Caso. Editor: Stephen Purvis.

Cast: Jonathan Emerson (LT), Nicholas Cascone (Easy), Jason Tomlins (Pretty Boy), Christopher Burgard (Hammer).

Summary: A two-man documentary crew accompanies a long-range reconnaissance patrol (LRRP) as they head into the bush. The camera (Mopic – motion picture) follows the platoon of five men as they travel through the jungle and end up engaging the enemy. None of the troopers are happy about the presence of the camera or the film-makers and eventually disaster strikes.

Subtext: A film that's as much about our experience of Vietnam as it is about the war, *Mopic* is a self-reflexive piece of film-making. Picking up on the fact that Vietnam was a war mediated by images and a war that was already a movie before Hollywood had the courage to turn it into one, *Mopic* foregrounds issues of war and representation with a neat plot device (the camera crew) that extended the late-1980s attempt to bring a new authenticity to films about the war.

Background: Writer/director Patrick Duncan is a Vietnam veteran who had first-hand experience of the combat zone as an infantryman, claimed that he was deliberately trying to overcome the problems that *Platoon*'s anti-war action film stance had produced. While Stone's film made war look like fun even as it was professing its anti-war sentiments, *Mopic* uses its pseudo-documentary approach to thrust the audience into the heart of the action. Duncan is careful to ensure that almost all the action is seen through the Mopic 16mm lens, thereby ensuring our identification with the platoon as they talk directly into the camera. It's a clever strategy and one that is surprisingly effective despite the obvious contrivances that such a situation necessarily produces. Duncan, who wrote and produced segments of HBO's *Vietnam War Story* series (1989-1990), used a grant from the Sundance Institute to get the film off the ground, giving this a slightly different feel that the usual Hollywood studio pictures about the war. Blending authentic dialogue and action with the central plot device of the camera crew, *Mopic* is one of the most original takes on the war—it's a shame then that it gets dragged off course by some heavy-handed plotting. As soon as 'Mopic' tells the story about camera footage returning from the battlefield without the cameraman you just know that tragedy is going to strike sooner or later.

Casualties Of War (1989)

Crew: Director: Brian De Palma. Producer: Art Linson. Writer: David Rabe, based on a *New Yorker* article and book by Daniel Lang. Cinematographer: Stephen H Burum. Editor: Bill Pankow.

Cast: Michael J Fox (Sven Eriksson), Sean Penn (Tony Meserve), Don Harvey (Clark), John C Reilly (Hatcher).

Summary: Squad Sergeant Meserve flips, kidnaps a local Vietnamese girl and encourages his squad to gang-rape her. Ignoring the objections of new guy Eriksson, the squad ultimately kills her. When they return to base Eriksson tries to tell his superior officers, but they're not interested. After surviving an assassination attempt by Meserve, Eriksson brings charges against the squad and justice is served.

Subtext: Casualties Of War treats the kidnapping, brutalisation and rape of the Vietnamese woman as a metaphor for the conflict itself. In addition, it raises questions about the bond that exists between fighting men. United in warfare, the men sublimate their feelings—in particular Meserve's anger and sorrow over the death of his friend Brown—and use the rape as a drastic means of mediating their relationships with one another. Eriksson's refusal to take part in the gang rape leads to his dismissal as a homosexual.

Background: Filmed in the wake of *Platoon, Casualties Of War* is a worthy attempt to breathe life back into the near-dead combat film by confronting the American catalogue of war atrocities head-on. Brian De Palma, an unlikely choice for such a blatant 'liberal conscience' movie, crafts a harrowing story of rape and war crimes from ex-grunt David Rabe's screenplay, but the overall effect is strangely muddled.

Following *Platoon*'s simplistic good/evil dichotomy between Elias and Barnes, *Casualties* sets Michael J Fox's liberal 'cherry' against Penn's clearly insane sergeant Meserve (a telling name if there ever was one). But of the two, it's actually Fox's private who comes off looking the worse. The film's far less interested in Meserve's inhumanity than it is in Eriksson's failure to do anything. For all his high and mighty sentiments, Eriksson doesn't help the victimized girl and it's a guilty burden that follows him well after the war as the opening and closing 'back in the world' sequences demonstrate. In the face of his wishy-washy liberalism and its cowardly impotence, the old Second World War cliché about evil triumphing if good people do nothing never seemed more apt.

But for all its anger, *Casualties Of War* never transcends the sum of its very derivative parts. De Palma is a director familiar with the Vietnam conflict (two films from his early days as a low-budget filmmaker—the rarely seen *Greetings* and *Hi Mom!*—take a satirical swipe at Vietnam), but in *Casualties Of War* he never manages to break out of the studio conventions that having big name stars like Penn and Fox foists upon him. The court martial scene, filmed almost entirely from the point of view of the anonymous authorities, deliberately tries to offer a simple solution to a complex problem by dispensing lengthy prison sentences to the rapists and paving the way for Fox's post-Nam encounter with an Asian girl who assures him that "it's over now, I think." The failure of good men to act, both in Vietnam and—on the basis of the black lieutenant's speech about Texas racism—back home, is whitewashed by the film's happy ending.

Tigerland (2000)

Crew: Director: Joel Schumacher. Producers: Arnon Milchan, Steven Hart, Beau Flynn. Writers: Ross Klavan, Michael McGruther. Cinematographer: Matthew Libatique. Editor: Mark Stevens.

Cast: Colin Farrell (Bozz), Matthew Collins (Paxton), Clifton Collins Jr. (Miter), Thomas Guiry (Cantwell), Shea Whigham (Wilson).

Summary: 1971 Fort Polk, Louisiana. After having been through their basic training a squad of infantry recruits destined for Vietnam begin their eight weeks of combat training. Private Bozz has a reputation as a troublemaker. He's deliberately broken every rule, ignored every command and subverted every form of military procedure he can and no amount of punishment duties, imprisonments or beatings seem to have any effect. During the course of the film he helps three recruits get a discharge from the army and then sacrifices his own chance of escape to save his friend Paxton from Vietnam.

Subtext: Taking the first segment of *Full Metal Jacket* as its starting point, *Tigerland* updates the boot camp movie for the post-Vietnam generation. Set during the tail end of the war in 1971, the film's characters are demotivated, disillusioned draftees who have no faith in either the war or the military's ability to win it. As one commander complains: "When did 'my country right or wrong' turn into 'fuck this shit'?" The impact of the 1960s has meant that every GI now knows more reasons not to fight than to pick up a weapon.

Background: Directed by Joel Schumacher, whose previous projects have included such crimes against cinema as *Batman & Robin*, *Tigerland* is a surprisingly adult movie that might have come from some unheard of first-time indie director rather than an old-hand 'high concept' director. Mixing anti-authoritarianism with a dark streak of pessimism, *Tigerland* occupies a self-consciously anti-war position. Yet it also has hidden depths. The script has an excellent sense of the class issues that surrounded the draft (almost everyone here is either poor white trash or black and the only college education trooper is an enlisted man who's signed up in the hope of gaining some literary experience.

What's more, the film also teases out the frustration and sheer despair that had engulfed America and the nation's military by 1971—the discontent that Bozz stirs up amongst his fellow troopers is clearly a result of the overwhelming sense that Vietnam is a waste of life. As his superiors point out, Bozz is a born platoon leader—generous, levelheaded and concerned about the welfare of his fellow men—but he has no stomach for a war in which civilians are being killed or for an army in which the recruits are taught how to use a standard infantry radio as a device for genital torture. What *Tigerland* recognizes is that by 1971, Vietnam had degenerated into a bloodbath where only psychopaths and baby killers could flourish and any hope of military service with honour had long since been shelled into a distant memory.

34

3. "This Is This": The Vet Movie

Somewhat surprisingly, the majority of the first films that directly dealt with Vietnam focused on veterans. Since military equipment was scarce during the 1960s and 1970s, many film-makers found that their dreams of making low-budget combat films were logistically impossible, never mind the fact that their audiences were so fed up with the televised war that they weren't particularly interested in seeing a second-hand version of it in the drive-ins or movie theatres. In comparison films about returning vets and their crazed antics were cheap to produce and often had enough lurid potential to guarantee an audience.

The exploitation film market developed in the wake of the Second World War, coming into its own in the 1950s and 1960s. Low-budget film-makers, and even mainstream Hollywood directors, had been obsessed with features about bikers, delinquents and beatniks ever since *The Wild One* had proved to be such an unexpected success. With plenty of room for sex and violence (and violence and sex) these films were guaranteed to turn a profit.

Vietnam proved a godsend to the exploitation film market. Stories about returning vets could be made on a shoestring budget, requiring little or no 'in country' scenes and giving scriptwriters instant justification for their main character's troubled and violent behaviour. The unexpected success of Tom Laughlin's *Billy Jack* series in the 1970s laid the groundwork for hundreds of features about returning combat troops among a few of which were *Chrome And Hot Leather* (1971), *Vigilante Force* (1976), *Rolling Thunder* (1977). Even other exploitation markets such as blaxploitation got in on the act with various films about African-American veterans (*Black Gunn*, 1972; *Slaughter*, 1972; *Slaughter's Big Ripoff*, 1973; and the deliriously weird vet/horror/blaxploitation hybrid *Blackenstein*, 1972).

Almost all of these films were disposable low-budget productions with few stars or famous directors—with some exceptions: the low-budget *The Visitors*, for instance, was helmed by no less than Elia Kazan. Most focused on psychologically rather than physically crippled veterans and their propensity for violence. Perhaps their popularity stemmed from the cruel quirk of history that meant that Vietnam was one of the first wars which wasn't followed by wild partying (because America hadn't won). Both World Wars had been followed by a riotous period of celebration—the Roaring Twenties and the consumerist boom of the 1950s. Vietnam was unique in that it was being fought *while* America partied. As troops humped the boonies in the 'Nam, their counterparts back home were turning on, tuning in and dropping out in a psychedelic party scene of drugs, free love and day-glo colours. How could anyone be surprised that the returning vets were being portrayed as being pissed off? Perhaps the vet films had a cathartic effect—on some level they gave the stay-at-home audience the opportunity to shed some of their collective guilt about sending these boys off to fight by letting them identify with the angry vet for ninety minutes.

After 1977, when mainstream Hollywood revamped the combat film, the vet movies were overshadowed by stories set 'in country', although they never disappeared entirely. In the same year, *Coming Home* became the first mainstream, award-winning film to deal with the vet issue and even in the 1980s, veterans could be found in everything from *First Blood* to *Lethal Weapon* to the horror comedy *House*. When Oliver Stone decided to return to Vietnam after his combat film *Platoon*, he significantly chose a vet-focused story, *Born On The Fourth Of July*, to get his anti-war views across.

Yet, although the vet movie had a glorious, thirty-year history, they've become increasingly scarce. As most vets are now somewhat too old to be credible action heroes, the vet movie may finally be at an end.

Billy Jack (1971)

Crew: Director: Tom Laughlin (as T C Frank). Producer: Tom Laughlin (as Mary Rose Solti). Writers: Tom Laughlin (as Frank Christina), Delores Taylor (as Teresa Christina). Cinematographer: Fred J Koenekamp. Editor: Larry Heath, Marion Rothman.

Cast: Tom Laughlin (Billy Jack), Delores Taylor (Jean Roberts), Clark Howat (Sheriff Cole), Victor Izay (Doctor).

Summary: Returning home from Vietnam, ex-Green Beret Billy Jack finds that his hometown is in conflict. The evil townsfolk are harassing the students at a nearby desert school, a kind of hippie commune prototype. Although he's desperate to leave violence aside, Billy Jack uses all his military training and karate skills to right the wrongs he sees around him.

Subtext: Half Native American Billy Jack is a born loser both because of his traumatic Vietnam experience and his racial background. But instead of accepting his outsider status, he uses his Green Beret training to stand up for himself and the townsfolk, fighting off the Hell's Angels and delivering justice. (No, it really is that shallow!).

Background: Billy Jack has a fascinating production history. The concept began life as a low-budget film that was only one step up from a home movie called *The Born Losers* (1967). The central character was a returning vet who comes home to find bikers and Hells Angels marauding through his town. Needless to say, the vet shows them the error of their ways.

Laughlin was sufficiently aware of its dubious technical quality to use a pseudonym for his director/producer credit (though vain enough to star under his own name) but by some quirk of cinematic history, *The Born Losers* proved to be successful in very, very modest terms but enough to convince Laughlin that he was onto something. A more expensive remake of the same story went into production as *Billy Jack*. Approached by Warner Bros., Laughlin agreed to let them distribute this new version of his movie. Sadly, the studio didn't invest much time or effort into their side of the contract and *Billy Jack* flopped. Laughlin had seen the success of *The Born Losers* and knew that *Billy Jack*'s mix of action and vets was what the public wanted so he sued Warner Bros., claiming that they hadn't marketed it properly. He then went on to distribute it himself, moving the print from cinema and promoting it in proportion to how much money it was taking at the box office. As a result, the *Billy Jack* series became one of the most successful low-budget franchises of the 1970s and set the pattern for stories about returning veterans.

The Visitors (1972)

Crew: Director: Elia Kazan. Producers: Chris Kazan, Nick Proferes. Writer: Chris Kazan. Cinematographer: Nick Proferes. Editor: Nick Proferes.

Cast: Patrick McVey (Harry Wayne), Patricia Joyce (Martha Wayne), James Woods (Bill Schmidt), Steve Railsback (Mike Nickerson), Chico Martinez (Tony Rodrigues).

Summary: Vietnam veteran Bill Schmidt lives on a farm with his girlfriend and their child. Mike and Tony, two of Bill's fellow vets, unexpectedly arrive, fresh from their stretch behind bars for the rape and murder of a Vietnamese girl during the war. Bill isn't overly pleased to see them since he testified against them at their trial. His girlfriend's father befriends the pair—even after he learns about the rape. They make themselves at home, flirt with Martha then beat up Bill and rape her.

Subtext: Martha's father is the most interesting character in the film—this Second World War veteran dislikes Bill's pacifism, casts doubt on his manliness and sexuality when he hears that Bill didn't want to take part in the rape and embraces the rapists as war heroes. The point about America civilians' vicarious enjoyment of the war and its horrors seems more than clear.

Background: Not even an esteemed director like Elia Kazan (best known for *On The Waterfront*) could find a studio that was willing to finance a drama about the impact of Vietnam in 1972. So, drumming up a minuscule $150,000 budget, he did the best he could on his own, relying on poor quality film stock and sound recording equipment, an unknown cast (with James Woods making his feature film debut) and a crew made up of friends and family. The final film stirred controversy at Cannes—where one jury member continued his long-running feud against Kazan because of his naming of names during the McCarthy hearings—and had a week-long theatrical release in New York before sinking without a trace. In the tradition of *Straw Dogs*, released the same year, the rape scenes are problematic since they implicitly suggest that the woman herself is responsible for the attack. Yet, as a symbol of America's war guilt coming back to haunt the nation during peacetime, the 'friendly' visitors (like prototypes of the sadists in *Funny Games*) are terrifyingly effective.

Brian De Palma's *Casualties Of War* was obviously aware of this much earlier story, although De Palma's film is far less effective since the rape and its aftermath take place 'in country'. The fact that the war can invade and destroy the American home and hearth—even when it is apparently over—is what gives *The Visitors* its disturbing power.

Taxi Driver (1976)

Crew: Director: Martin Scorsese. Producers: Michael Phillips, Julia Phillips. Writer: Paul Schrader. Cinematographer: Michael Chapman. Editors: Marcia Lucas, Tom Rolf, Melvin Shapiro.

Cast: Robert De Niro (Travis Bickle), Cybill Shepherd (Betsy), Jodie Foster (Iris), Harvey Keitel (Sport).

Summary: Ex-marine Travis Bickle drives a cab around New York's streets on the night shift. Disgusted by the sex and drugs he sees around him he slowly begins to crack up. When political campaign worker Betsy dumps him, he vows to do "something." After a botched assassination attempt on Betsy's presidential candidate, Travis decides to help twelve-year-old prostitute Iris by killing her pimps.

Subtext: Of all the urban Westerns (like *The Warriors*, *Assault On Precinct Thirteen* and *Death Wish*) that were so popular in the 1970s, *Taxi Driver* is the most impressive. It wears its Western credentials on its sleeve—Travis is the cowboy (complete with uncool boots) to Sport's Indian (check out Keitel's mane of fake hair held in place with a bandanna). Just as Rambo becomes an Apache in *First Blood*, so Travis becomes the latter day Last Of The Mohicans (as his extreme hairstyle suggests), prompting Sport to tell him to "go back to your fucking tribe." In case the Western elements weren't obvious enough, the film's set-up is loosely based on John Ford's *The Searchers* (1956) in which the racist cowboy Ethan (John Wayne) fights to rescue his niece from the Comanches.

Background: Taxi Driver is the most well known and critically acclaimed of the films discussed in this chapter, a milestone of 1970s cinema. Yet, it's also the one film that's rarely given its due as a Vietnam veteran's film. Critics and film fans often talk about the movie in the context of *film noir* and Scorsese's obsession with the mean streets of the city, but this is usually at the expense of seeing *Taxi Driver* as the apotheosis of the veterans' cycle. Admittedly, there are few explicit references to the war: there are no flashbacks, no mention of combat experience and no scenes set 'in country' (the suggestion that Travis is a vet is almost subliminal—he mentions being an ex-marine and wears an army issue jacket bearing the insignia of the 'King Kong' company). These subtle hints—added to Travis' weapons training, insomnia and psychosis—have a cumulative effect. Travis is the ultimate Vietnam vet, completely psychotic, completely dispossessed. As Betsy says, he's a "walking contradiction," a peep show voyeur who wants to wash all the scum off the street; the spectre of Vietnam come back to haunt New York's night streets; a living reproach of the city's immorality and political bankruptcy (Senator Pallantine's speech includes the line "we the people who suffered in Vietnam," but somehow you guess he probably spent the war in Canada along with Bill Clinton). He is, as Iris' malapropism suggests, a vengeful scorpion (rather than a Scorpio) with a sting in his tail that he's itching to use.

More than any other Vietnam vet film, *Taxi Driver* manages to match its visual style to the central character's psychosis. The film's editing, lighting and camera angles are infected by Travis' fractured vision, from the off-kilter slow motion sequences, use of overhead shots (including the celebrated dolly shot that moves across the ceiling of Iris' room after the gun battle), out of synch soundtrack and red camera lenses. And, of course, that final speeded-up psychotic shot of Travis looking into his rear-view mirror is one of the most chilling sequences in cinema history. The rear-view mirror is the film's most subtle index of Travis' mental state—he is after all a man who's always looking backwards—to the war.

The Deer Hunter (1978)

Crew: Director: Michael Cimino. Producers: Barry Spikings, Michael Deeley, Michael Cimino, John Peverall. Writer: Deric Washburn. Cinematographer: Vilmos Zgismond. Editor: Peter Zinner.

Cast: Robert De Niro (Michael), John Cazale (Stan), John Savage (Steve), Christopher Walken (Nick), Meryll Streep (Linda).

Summary: As three Pennsylvania steelworkers prepare to ship out to Vietnam, one of them gets married and the rest go hunting in the hills above the town. After a brutal tour of duty—including a spell as POWs forced to play Russian Roulette—their lives are shattered. Steve returns home in a wheelchair; Michael begins to question his fascination with the violence of the hunt; and Nick is so traumatized by the VC's torture that he continues playing Russian roulette for money in Saigon. Michael returns to save him, but Nick shoots himself in the head. Back in America Michael and the rest of his friends reunite at Nick's funeral.

Subtext: While *The Green Berets* used the Western genre as a point of reference for its overly simplistic understanding of the war as a battle between cowboys and Indians, *The Deer Hunter* deliberately styles itself around the mythic themes of the Western—masculinity, the relationship between the individual and the community and the self-reliance of the frontier. Michael is a loner, a frontiersman who is happiest in the wilderness. He's a man's man who detests the false machismo of mouthy Stan (who carries a snub-nosed revolver around for "protection") and who believes in the ethic of "one shot"—the supreme proof of a man's virility. Joining the army becomes an extension of Michael's love of the wilderness. Not only does he join the Rangers (quite symbolic), but he proves his ability to survive in a harsh environment, battling the local inhabitants (read Native Americans) and escaping from captivity like some Puritan American settler. Much like Natty Bumppo in James Fenimore Cooper's novel *The Last Of The Mohicans* (1826), Michael is a man who's always destined to be excluded from life in the civilized town, but whose free spirit is able to reunite the townsfolk and regenerate the community (even though he fails to save Nick, Michael brings Steve back into the community and cements the relationships between all the friends).

Background: Released in the same year as *Coming Home, The Deer Hunter* caused quite a sensation when it first opened in cinemas. At the Oscars it won awards for Best Picture, Director and Supporting Actor (Christopher Walken) even as a debate raged about whether or not it was racist. Certainly, Cimino's portrayal of the Vietnamese is far from sympathetic; they are predominantly styled as a braying bunch of savages (there was never any evidence that the VC forced prisoners to play Russian Roulette—it's an image that Cimino obviously felt was artistically correct if not historically accurate).

But, whatever reservations audiences had about the film's racial politics, *The Deer Hunter* clearly deserved the Best Picture Oscar if only because of its stunning artistry (its main competitor, *Coming Home*, was far inferior). Zgismond's stunning photography, Stanley Myers' haunting score and the terrific performances combine to make *The Deer Hunter* one of the greatest films ever to have been made about Vietnam.

The Exterminator (1980)

Crew: Director: James Glickenhaus. Producers: Lester Berman, Mark Buntzman. Writer: James Glickenhaus. Cinematographer: Robert M Baldwin. Editor: Corky O'Hara.

Cast: Robert Ginty (John Eastland), Christopher George (James Dalton), Samantha Eggar (Megan Stewart), Steve James (Michael Jefferson).

Summary: Returning from a tour of duty in Vietnam, John and Michael get jobs in New York's meat-packing district. When they encounter a gang of thugs robbing one of the local warehouses they use their combat skills to fight them off. The next day the gang beat up Michael, leaving him paralysed. John swears revenge on them and the rest of the city's criminals and becomes a vigilante. The CIA fear that his actions may be part of a conspiracy to damage the upcoming mayoral elections and so try to assassinate him, but instead they kill the policeman who's been chasing him. The Exterminator survives for the requisite sequel option.

Subtext: The interracial friendship between John and Michael is the only thing that's vaguely liberal in this picture. The rest of the film is reactionary hogwash—writer-director Glickenhaus implies that the junkies, dopers and muggers of 1980s New York don't deserve the freedom that vets like John and Michael fought for.

Background: A pure exploitation picture, *The Exterminator* is the kind of low-budget, inept production that would today be classified as Z-grade entertainment. It's pretty charmless stuff. For all his supposed combat experience (bits and pieces of which crop up throughout the film in flashback) Ginty is an unlikely action hero, with a jaw that's less chiselled than missing (eagle-eyed viewers may remember seeing him as Bob Hyde's comrade in arms in *Coming Home*). The sub-*Taxi Driver* milieu of brothels, sex shows and Times Square hookers is hackneyed, as is John's justification for his actions: "It was like we were back in 'Nam," he tells his paralysed brother-in-arms after executing the first gang member, "It didn't matter if it was right or wrong, I just did it."

More interesting is the array of weaponry and ingenious methods of dispatching his victims that John employs. One mafia boss is fed into a meat grinder, gang members are left to the rats and several are threatened with The Exterminator's rather nasty flame-thrower (purging the city of evil with his purifying fire, eh?). The flame-thrower was enough of a crowd pleaser to become the vigilante's weapon of choice in the sequel.

Slightly more interesting is the film's half-hearted allusion to the bureaucrats who (allegedly) lost the war. The CIA operatives sent out to catch the vigilante fear that he may be an agent of a foreign government or some domestic party desperate to scupper the city's imminent elections. The policeman tracking the vigilante is amazed at how out of touch the CIA men really are—just as grunts in the 'Nam complained about the ignorance of senior officers and pencil pushers. But the symbolism is clear. "Washington will be pleased," say the CIA operatives after assassinating both the cop and (they mistakenly think) the vigilante. Just as in 'Nam, it's the troops on the ground who understand the realities of the battle against gooks or crooks and, as *The Exterminator* takes pains to show, they should be left to fight the good fight without interference from know-nothing eggheads in Washington. The fact that Ginty is running around the streets of New York with a flame-thrower doesn't seem to matter in Glickenhaus' scheme of things.

First Blood (1982)

Crew: Director: Ted Kotcheff. Producer: Buzz Feitshans. Writers: Michael Kozoll, William Sackheim, Sylvester Stallone, based on the novel by David Morrell. Cinematographer: Andrew Lazlo. Editor: Joan Chapman.

Cast: Sylvester Stallone (John Rambo), Richard Crenna (Colonel Trautman) Brian Dennehy (Sheriff Will Teasle), David Caruso (Mitch).

Summary: Special Forces veteran John Rambo is arrested by a small-town sheriff. Mistreated by the local police, Rambo suffers flashbacks to his time in a Vietnam POW camp and escapes into the woods. The police pursue him but after one officer dies and the others are wounded they call in the National Guard who trap the fugitive in a cave. Special Forces Colonel Trautman arrives and tells the sheriff about Rambo's military background. Rambo escapes the mine and returns to the town. Trautman manages to stop him from killing the sheriff. Sobbing, Rambo tells Trautman about his post-traumatic stress.

Subtext: In his one-man guerrilla war against the well-equipped police force, Rambo is like the VC fighting the Vietnam army. As film critic Rick Berg suggests, the vet becomes the Vet Cong. Picking off his pursuers one by one, Rambo uses his survival training and a series of primitive weapons (spears and punji sticks). The film also borrows the imagery of the Western—Rambo's bare-chested, bandanna-wearing pose makes him look like a marauding Apache Indian (to make sure we don't miss this pointed analogy, the script mentions that Rambo is also half-Native American).

Background: Based on the novel by David Morrell, *First Blood* is at once an excellent action film and a telling dramatisation of America's treatment of its war veterans. Sylvester Stallone's monosyllabic mus-cleman may well be a Special Forces superhero but the humiliation that he suffers at the hands of Dennehy's redneck sheriff is an image of the nation's rejection of the men it had sent to fight an unpopular war. *First Blood* wasn't the first veteran film to feature a rampaging hero, but it was the first of the subgenre to explicitly style the veteran's violence as a replay of the war itself. It was also the first film to try and seriously confront the issue of post-traumatic stress (no matter how fleetingly)—

Rambo's breakdown, as he collapses sobbing into the dazed Trautman's arms, is a surprisingly moving scene and one that's certainly not in keeping with the usual dynamics of a macho action film: most action films deal with emotional distress, if at all, at the beginning of the story, letting their characters find catharsis through violence—think of Mel Gibson's transformation from suicidal nutter to trusted friend and companion in *Lethal* Weapon for instance. As he rails against the world Rambo claims that American forces could have prevailed over the VC if they had been allowed to: "I did what I had to do to win—but somebody wouldn't let us win."

Sadly the sequels that cashed in on *First Blood*'s unexpected success reduced the finale's emotional depth to the level of comic strip superheroes and upped the script's reactionary politics—Rambo became a mechanical killing machine (something implicit in his name itself 'ram' 'bow') rather than a tortured victim of America's incompetent handling of the returning veterans.

Gardens Of Stone (1987)

Crew: Director: Francis Ford Coppola. Producers: Michael I Levy, Francis Ford Coppola. Writer: Ronald Bass, based on the novel by Nicholas Proffitt. Cinematographer: Jordan Cronenweth. Editor: Barry Malkin.

Cast: James Caan (Sergeant Hazard), Anjelica Huston (Samantha), James Earl Jones (Sergeant Goody Nelson), DB Sweeney (Jackie Willow).

Summary: At Arlington military cemetery, Sergeants Hazard and Nelson are part of the Honor Guard responsible for burying the dead. Both are veterans of Korea who believe that they could teach the recruits at Fort Benning how to survive in Vietnam, but their superior officer won't give them a transfer. An old friend asks them to look after their son, Willow, who joins their unit. He's gung-ho and ready for combat but Hazard tries to calm him down. When Willow dies in Vietnam, Hazard is distraught.

Subtext: Sergeant Hazard is the tough but fair patriarchal figure whose inability to save even one soldier (Willow) highlights the differ-

45

ence between Vietnam and earlier wars (Korea, the Second World War) and also underscores the fact that the majority of combat troops in Vietnam were young, fresh-faced and largely inexperienced boys.

Background: One of the more curious films in the Vietnam War genre, *Gardens Of Stone* is somewhat unclassifiable. It's not a combat film (there's only one scene set 'in country' and that's in the form of television footage), yet it's about combat. It's not a protest film (the whole issue of the anti-war peace movement is touched on only in passing), yet it's decidedly anti-war. It's not a vet film, but it's about two veterans from earlier wars and the impact of the Vietnam War. So what is it? The answer is (at the risk of being awkward) all three.

Coppola's second foray into the world of Vietnam is in complete contrast to the surrealism of *Apocalypse Now*; *Gardens Of Stone* is probably the most sombre and sober Vietnam War film after *The Deer Hunter*. Yet, despite the fact that it's an anti-war film, *Gardens Of Stone* is so obsessed with the military that it verges on being reactionary. Filmed with the American army's help (they approved the script since it showed the military in a good light, unlike *Apocalypse Now*), *Gardens Of Stone* is something of a hymn to the rituals and traditions of military ceremony—so much so that the army gave Coppola a 'Certificate of Appreciation for Patriotic Civilian Service'—as well as a requiem for the death of American boys during the war (Coppola's own son, Gio, died in a boating accident just before filming began). It's a film that celebrates the army as an extended family, while mourning the loss of so many of that family's members during the war years. Beautifully shot, wonderfully acted (Caan and Jones' performances offer a truly outstanding sense of military camaraderie), *Gardens Of Stone* remains one of the most problematic films to have come out of the war—part pro-military, part peacenik, 100% pro-American.

Jacknife (1988)

Crew: Director: David Jones. Producers: Robert Schaffel, Carol Baum. Writer: Stephen Metcalfe based on his play *Strange Snow*. Cinematographer: Brian West. Editor: John Bloom.

Cast: Robert De Niro (Megs), Ed Harris (Dave), Kathy Baker (Martha), Charles Dutton (Jake).

Summary: When Vietnam veteran Megs tracks down his old comrade Dave, he discovers that his buddy has become a morose alcoholic. Attracted by Dave's schoolteacher sister Martha and eager to help his friend put the war behind him, Megs becomes involved in both their lives, dating Martha and desperately trying to curb Dave's self-destructive behaviour. But as a series of 'Nam flashbacks show, Dave still blames Megs for the death of their friend Bobby; only by confronting the past together can they hope to face the future.

Subtext: Proclaiming himself a knight in shining armour, Megs is destined to be the salvation of both Dave and Martha. Through his intervention the brother and sister are rejuvenated. Martha is transformed from dowdy housewife to queen of the prom and Dave is encouraged to replace the beer bottle with group therapy sessions at the local veterans' centre.

Background: Based on a stage play by Stephen Metcalfe entitled *Strange Snow*, *Jacknife* is a slow-burning drama about veterans and the legacy of Vietnam. While most veterans films start with an explosive action sequence set 'in country', *Jacknife* opens with an equally explosive, rapid-fire domestic scene in which Megs invades Dave's house to wake him up for opening day. It's a lively sequence that's held together—like most of the film—by De Niro's shambling performance as the eccentric but well-meaning Megs.

Refusing to glamorise its stars or its story (Harris and De Niro sport tatty facial hair and every scene takes place on dank, dreary sets), *Jacknife* is an honest, if slight, story about post-traumatic stress. Ed Harris' Dave is a self-destructive loser, drinking and drugging himself into oblivion, picking fights with college kids wearing combat gear and slowly losing the plot. The 'in country' sequences explain the guilt and blame motivating the post-war Megs/Dave relationship—Megs ("Jacknife") used to be crazily gung-ho and Dave blames him for the death of their friend Bobby (although it was actually Dave's cowardice and resulting leg injury that contributed to Bobby getting shot).

It's a performance-led film, with Harris and Baker doing their best to match De Niro's central turn. Apart from a throwaway reference to the fact that Dave enlisted (while Megs was a draftee), there's little attempt to deal with the social forces that contributed to the war—like so many Vietnam War films, *Jacknife* is ultimately interested in the personal story of its characters rather than the bigger picture.

Distant Thunder (1988)

Crew: Director: Rick Rosenthal. Producer: Robert Schaffel. Writers: Robert Stitzel, Deedee Wehle. Cinematographer: Ralf Bode. Editor: Dennis Virkler.

Cast: John Lithgow (Mark Lambert), Ralph Macchio (Jack Lambert), Kerrie Keane (Char), Reb Brown (Harvey Nitz), Denis Arndt (Larry).

Summary: Navy SEAL Vietnam veteran Mark Lambert lives in the forests of the Pacific Northwest with a group of other 'bush vets' who have dropped out of mainstream society. Finding work at the local logging factory, Mark is befriended by Char who encourages him to contact his eighteen-year-old son Jack whom he hasn't seen since he was a baby. Jack comes to find his father in the forest, but their initial meeting is fraught with tension. Meanwhile, Char's boyfriend Larry has become jealous and tracks them into the forest. He's attacked by one of the other veterans, Nitz, who goes on the rampage. Mark manages to subdue Nitz and rescues Larry. Mark's so distraught that he tries to commit suicide, but his son saves him.

Subtext: Essentially a melodrama about a father and son's relationship, *Distant Thunder* makes young Jack relive his father's 'Nam experiences. Seeing Larry get stabbed and another vet get his head blown off by a shotgun gives Jack a little taste of why his father has been hiding in the forest for the last decade.

Background: A late entry in the Vietnam Vet cycle, *Distant Thunder* clearly marks the tail end of the subgenre. By 1987, vets were so commonplace that they'd begun to crop up in mainstream action movies like

Lethal Weapon and *Distant Thunder* loses its thunder by the over-familiarity of Lithgow's troubled veteran. As a result, the true story of America's 'bush vets' is turned into cheap melodrama. While Lithgow's hero is merely troubled (maintaining a distinct gravitas throughout), his fellow vets Nitz and Moss are clearly loony tunes, one a psychopath the other a gummy bear munching halfwit. The film's central message appears to be that being traumatized is fine as long as one's ready to be reintegrated back into normal society. Living in the woods, making pitfall traps and living off a constant diet of candy bars is just too weird to be forgiven—Mark's clearly the only vet who's going to get rehabilitated. Combine this with second-hand flashbacks and unconvincing dialogue—"It's so hard to explain what all of us went through," Mark tells his son; "What about what I went through?" is the me-generation brat's reply—and you've got a below par B-movie that's destined for video rental oblivion (much like Ralph 'The Karate Kid' Macchio's subsequent career). Lithgow deserved much better.

Born On The Fourth Of July (1989)

Crew: Director: Oliver Stone. Producers: A Kitman Ho, Oliver Stone. Writers: Oliver Stone, Ron Kovic, based on the book by Kovic. Cinematographer: Robert Richardson. Editor: David Brenner.

Cast: Tom Cruise (Ron Kovic), Kyra Sedgwick (Donna), Raymond J Barry (Mr Kovic), Willem Dafoe (Charlie).

Summary: 1963. High school graduate Ron Kovic decides to join the Marines and see action in Vietnam. Once 'in country' he witnesses an accidental massacre and, during combat, shoots one of his own men. Later he's wounded and is shipped back to the States. In the veterans' hospital, Kovic learns that he's paralyzed and will have to use a wheelchair for the rest of his life. He returns home to live with his family, becomes a drunk, flees to a life of whoring in Mexico and then returns to the States to join the anti-war protestors. He becomes a leading member of the anti-war movement.

Subtext: Born On The Fourth of July draws parallels between the body and the body politic. After Kovic is wounded in action he is symbolically castrated by his injuries: "I'm not whole—I'll never be."

America suffers the same fate because of the Vietnam War—a fragmented nation torn apart by demonstrations, student riots and the loss of a whole generation of young men in Vietnam's rice paddies. Kovic's transformation from bitter cripple to committed political leader prefigures America's own redemption and the healing of the nation's wounds.

Background: The second instalment in Oliver Stone's trilogy about the Vietnam War, sandwiched between the combat scenes of *Platoon* and the feminist posturing of *Heaven & Earth*, *Born On The Fourth Of July* probably deserves to be regarded as one of the director's best works. The autobiographical story of Ron Kovic serves as a metaphor for America's experience of the war and its aftermath. Kovic—born on America's birthday of Independence Day, July 4th—suffers through America's injuries and ultimate redemption. As the film opens he's gung-ho. He believes the lecture that Tom Berenger's Marine Sergeant gives the class, he buys Kennedy's line about "ask not what your country can do for you but what you can do for your country" and he finds that the price for such trust in such "bullshit lies" is disillusionment and disfigurement. As in *Platoon*, the central character is forced to go from innocence to experience in order to find redemption—by the end of the film Kovic says, "We're home. I think maybe we're home," as he wheels himself on stage to address the crowd.

Closely tied to these ideas about the nation is the issue of masculinity. Kovic is feminized because of the war and his injuries, losing his male prowess just as America lost its military security. Although he begins the film smothered by his overbearing mother, Kovic is ultimately able to re-masculinize himself and America itself by engaging with politics. His flight to Mexico is self-indulgent and ultimately cowardly—it's only when he returns to America and goes into battle again, this time in the fight for an end to the war, that he's able to rediscover his identity as an American. Unlike his emotional but slightly henpecked father, Kovic proves his masculinity by struggling onwards in the face of adversity and never losing sight of the fact that the price of victory is sacrifice.

In Country (1989)

Crew: Director: Norman Jewison. Producers: Norman Jewison, Richard Roth. Writers: Frank Pierson, Cynthia Cidre, based on the novel by Bobbie Ann Mason. Cinematographer: Russell Boyd. Editors: Antony Gills, Lou Lombardo

Cast: Bruce Willis (Emmett Smith), Emily Lloyd (Samantha Hughes), Joan Allen (Irene), Kevin Anderson (Lonnie).

Summary: Teenager Samantha lives with her Uncle Emmett, a Vietnam veteran. Her father died in the war just a few weeks after she was born and she's eager to understand what happened out there, but none of the vets want to tell her about it and the rest of the town act as if there never was a war. When she finds some of her father's old letters she dumps her boyfriend, has a brief fling with one of the vets and then convinces Emmett and her grandma to journey out to the Washington Vietnam Veterans Memorial where they find her daddy's name and pay their respects.

Subtext: Samantha's ignorance about the war—she calls Bouncing Betty mines "Bouncing Boobies" and is shocked by stories about American soldiers collecting the ears of dead Vietnamese—is supposed to be indicative of her generation's attitude to anything that happened before 1980. Yet her inquisitiveness puts the non-combatants to shame—the rest of the townsfolk just want to forget that the war ever happened.

Background: Trying to discover the truth about the war—and the impossibility of ever doing that—is the central theme of *In Country*. While most films in the veterans cycle hinge on the moment when the traumatized/crazy/sick veteran actually spills his guts about what happened to him 'in country', the point of Bobbie Ann Mason's novel is that such knowledge for those of us born after the war (or who stayed at home) is impossible. "You weren't there so you can't understand it," her uncle tells her several times. No matter how many letters or diaries she reads and no matter how many photographs she stares at, the war will always be unknowable.

What a shame, then, that director Jewison throws in a series of silly flashbacks sequences that undermine the audience's sense of just how unknowable the war is. Sadly, it's just one of many travesties—

51

Mason's novel deserved much better than Lloyd's annoying overacting and Willis' somnambulistic performance. There's much made of the usual we-could-have-won nonsense—"We could've paved that motherfucker over and put a McDonald's right in the middle of it if they would have let us" says one character—and the subtleties of Mason's novels are nowhere to be seen. The final scenes, set in Washington, capture the strangeness of America's memorial to its fallen soldiers, a huge wall of black marble carved out of the ground like some enormous mass grave. In real life, as in the film, its design caused a great deal of controversy.

4. "Charlie Don't Surf!":

Drugs And Surrealism In The Combat Zone

In 1975, after American troops had withdrawn from Vietnam and the fall of Saigon was imminent, South Vietnamese helicopter pilots ditched their half-a-million-dollar helicopters into the ocean so that they didn't fall into Communist hands. It was a surreal moment that characterized the whole war. Hovering above the water, the pilots leapt out of the cockpit and swam to safety as the helicopters crashed into the sea. A nearby American aircraft carrier which oversaw the action but was too overloaded to carry the choppers back home, picked the pilots out of the water. As a final image of the war—broadcast on network television back in the US—the sinking helicopters were a fitting symbol of Vietnam's utter pointlessness.

If the war in Vietnam was surreal, it was also a surrealism that was at least partly fuelled by drugs. More than any other conflict in history, Vietnam—or at least the Americans' experience of it—was dominated by all manner of narcotics, marijuana, heroin and, of course, acid. Stories of drug taking in the two World Wars are rare but in Vietnam drugs were everywhere. Statistics from the conflict suggest that 80% of GIs smoked dope and 15% of vets returned with heroin habits that they'd started while out in South East Asia. As one vet claimed, "I was stoned everyday of my life in Vietnam … It was the only way to deal with all the horror and the insanity, and that's what everyone did. Everyone was stoned on something."

Films about the war have often foregrounded the prevalence of hallucinogens in the combat zone, with Henry Jaglom's *Tracks* and Coppola's *Apocalypse Now* bearing the distinction of being the first acid 'Nam films. Other movies have recognized the widespread use of drugs, with films like *Go Tell The Spartans*, *Hamburger Hill* and *Platoon* featuring drug taking to some degree or another. So much so that the sight of a GI with a joint has become a cliché.

The only films not to feature drug taking were the 'Return to 'Nam' films and many of the veterans movies. After all, it's hard to imagine

Rambo puffing on a joint (if only because the Reaganite ideology of the period was so rabidly anti-drugs). Many of the more exploitative veterans' films follow the same conservative line, with the avenging vet often taking on the city's drug dealers and addicts in an attempt to clean the place up (as in *Taxi Driver* and *The Exterminator*). But for other films, the secret history of drugs during the war has made the theme ripe for conspiracy movies such as *Jacob's Ladder* and even action blockbusters like *Air America*.

Rumours frequently circulated that the VC were deliberately flooding the army ranks with drugs in order to weaken the fighting potential of American servicemen. Whatever the truth behind these rumours, it's worth noting that the top brass of the American army were fairly complicit with the whole drug issue. No real attempts were made to stop pot smoking and the military's R&D technicians were making good use of psychedelics as weapons of war anyway. As Martin A Lee and Bruce Shlain argue in *Acid Dreams: The Complete Social History of LSD: The CIA, The Sixties and Beyond*, psychochemical warfare was high on the list of the Pentagon's priorities during the period and there were apparently several field tests of the super-hallucinogen 'BZ' (the drug mentioned in *Jacob's Ladder*) against the VC. Although the results of such field tests were none too positive (the drug was difficult to deploy in a combat situation), Lee and Shlain suggest that the army was enthusiastic enough about the drug to stockpile fifty tons of it. Enough "to turn everyone in the world into a stark raving lunatic."

Tracks (1976)

Crew: Director: Henry Jaglom. Producer: Bert Schneider. Writer: Henry Jaglom. Cinematographer: Paul Glickman. Editor: George Folsey Jnr.

Cast: Dennis Hopper (Jack Falen), Taryn Power (Stephanie), Dean Stockwell (Mark), Topo Swope (Chloe).

Summary: Vietnam veteran Sergeant Jack Falen is escorting a military coffin on a train across America. The train is full of bizarre characters—a counter-cultural radical, a government informer, a comely college girl—but none of these are quite as bizarre as Falen himself. He starts hallucinating—imagining that the passengers are raping and beating one another. These psychedelic visions continue until the end of the film where Falen finally loses control when no one turns up at the funeral of his buddy. He jumps into the grave and emerges armed to the teeth in full combat gear to take his revenge.

Subtext: Bearing the burden of guilt for having taken part in the fighting in Vietnam, Falen is really only searching for peace and forgiveness. Sadly, no one he meets is willing to help him put the war to rest. His name suggests that he may already be dead ('fallen') and has returned home as a ghost. The funeral that no one can be bothered attending might as well be his own—maybe that's why the coffin actually turns out not to have carried a body?

Background: Henry Jaglom's film highlights the relationship between the counter-cultural upheaval of the 1960s and early 1970s with the war in Vietnam. Searching for a visual style to emphasize his point, Jaglom creates the first acid Vietnam movie. Relying on a psychedelic visual style, disorientating editing and an unhinged central performance from Dennis Hopper, *Tracks* has become something of a cult classic: rarely seen but often talked about. While *Apocalypse Now* is a fairly conventional film that uses a series of surreal images to suggest a drug-addled vision of the conflict, *Tracks* takes the disorientated states of altered consciousness as its aesthetic starting point. It's a film that's playful, frustrating and exasperating in equal measures—it refuses to make sense, but delights in being weird. The final scene, in which Hopper's character leaps into the grave, opens the coffin and emerges armed and dressed in combat gear, has provoked different interpretations from critics.

Apocalypse Now (1979)

Crew: Director: Francis Ford Coppola. Producer: Francis Ford Coppola. Writers: John Milius, Francis Ford Coppola, based on Joseph Conrad's *Heart Of Darkness*. Cinematographer: Vittorio Storaro. Editor: Walter Murch, Richard Marks.

Cast: Martin Sheen (Captain Willard), Robert Duvall (Colonel Kilgore), Marlon Brando (Colonel Kurtz), Frederic Forrest (Chef), Dennis Hopper (Photojournalist).

Summary: Captain Willard is given a secret mission to assassinate a renegade colonel named Kurtz. Travelling to the Cambodian border on a river patrol boat, Willard and his escort witness a series of absurd and horrific incidents—including an Air Cavalry attack, a Playboy Bunnies show and a chaotic border outpost operating without a commanding officer. Willard finally finds Kurtz's compound and kills the Colonel.

Subtext: Explicitly based on Joseph Conrad's 1902 novella *Heart Of Darkness*—in which the narrator, Marlow, was sent up the Congo River in search of an ivory trader named Kurtz—*Apocalypse Now* is a mythic journey into the nightmare that was Vietnam and, less explicitly, the dark region of man's soul.

Background: The making of *Apocalypse Now* is almost as interesting as the film itself. Filmed in the Philippines jungle on a shoot that lasted over 200 days by a megalomaniac director, the huge budget spiralled further and further out of control, topping $30 million. *Apocalypse Now* was, as Coppola himself realized, a cinematic parallel to the war itself: "We were in the jungle, there were too many of us. We had access to too much money and too much equipment and little by little, we went insane." Rarely has a film so uniquely mirrored its subject.

The dominant theme of the film is the absurdity of the Vietnam War and its surreal futility. Re-imagining 'Nam as an operatic acid trip, Coppola ruthlessly pursued his war-as-drug-trip vision (one of the characters, Lance the surfer, even drops acid during a battle scene). The surreal episodes—such as Kilgore's Air Cavalry assault on a VC-held village simply because the nearby waves are reputedly good for surfing—serve to emphasize the fact that it was America's failure to deal with Vietnam on its own terms that made the war so absurd. Instead of accepting the foreign nature of the country, the American forces tried to take the USA into the jungle with them, by ordering in T-Bones and Budweisers and airlifting in Playboy Bunnies to entertain the grunts. Only Kurtz and Willard realize the futility of this tactic. They see "the horror" clearly enough to understand that no amount of empty symbols from the land back home can disguise the reality of the war and America's imperialist involvement in Vietnam.

The final section of the film, set in Kurtz's compound, has as much to do with metaphysics and morality as drugs. *Apocalypse Now* is more than just a war film; it's meditation on the nature of humanity. John Milius' original screenplay had ended with an action sequence that saw Kurtz and Willard join forces to defend the camp from attack, but Coppola dropped this in favour of the assassination. Wearing a variety of anthropological and literary sources on its sleeve (everything from Weston's *From Ritual To Romance* to TS Eliot's 'Hollow Men'), the final section of the film gives Kurtz's death a mythic significance far beyond the death of some renegade Colonel. What Coppola tries to give us—and critics have always remained divided on whether he succeeds or not—is a glimpse into the dark heart of humanity itself to the accompaniment of Wagner and the thud, thud, thud of helicopter rotor blades. Vietnam and Metaphysics for the post-acid MTV generation.

Apocalypse Now Redux (2001)

Essentially the same film as *Apocalypse Now*, but with an extra forty-nine minutes of footage that was previously unseen, *Apocalypse Now Redux* deserves a separate entry because its change in tone is drastic enough to alter the emphasis of the original film. The most striking addition in terms of footage is the French Plantation scene, in which Willard and the crew eat an impromptu dinner with a group of French colonialists. In terms of the Vietnam War, this scene is vital to *Apocalypse Now*'s historical understanding of the conflict as a war that raged long before the 1960s with the defeat of the French at Điên Biên Phủ in 1954. These remnants of the colonial era, adrift in time, give the film an added perspective on the war. The rest of the footage is smattered throughout the film and mostly adds an extra depth to Willard's relationship with the crew—there are also additional scenes inside Kurtz's compound with more of Brando's improvisational ramblings about life, death and art, though the less said about these the better—transforming him from an alienated loner into something more human. This humanity is enhanced by the French plantation sequence, which includes a love scene and is negated in the additional Playboy Bunny scene in which Willard buys the crew sex with the Playmate of the Year in exchange for fuel.

The result is a film that's slightly less dark than the original version, with more humorous asides—Willard stealing Kilgore's surfboard, for instance; or sharing in the crew's banter—that soften the existential angst that characterized the original film. Whether or not it deserved a cinema release in today's age of DVD extras and scene hopping is a moot point, but then, considering the fact that *Apocalypse Now* very nearly bankrupted its director, it's easy to understand why Coppola might feel justified in milking this cash cow for as many dollars as is humanly possible.

Good Morning Vietnam (1987)

Crew: Director: Barry Levinson. Producers: Mark Johnson, Larry Brezner. Writer: Mitch Markowitz. Cinematographer: Peter Sova. Editor: Stu Linder.

Cast: Robin Williams (Adrian Cronauer), Forrest Whitaker (Edward Garlick), Tung Thanh Tran (Tuan), J T Walsh (Sergeant Major Dickerson).

Summary: Airman Adrian Cronauer is sent to Vietnam in 1965 to join Saigon's Armed Forces Radio. He discovers that his brand of humour and irreverence isn't appreciated by his superiors, but is loved by the troops in the field. Cronauer becomes involved with a Vietnamese girl and her brother Tran. After a VC terrorist bombing in Saigon Cronauer breaks army regulations by reading uncensored news of the bombing on the radio. Later Cronauer discovers that Tran was responsible for the bombing. Accused of fraternizing with the enemy, Cronauer is shipped out of Vietnam.

Subtext: Cronauer's irreverent, anarchic comedy is set off against the uptight, anally-retentive military authorities who can't deal with anything that falls outside of the Army's rulebooks. As the war in Vietnam escalates (the film begins at the relatively early date of 1965), Cronauer's madcap antics seem to be the only response in a world that's clearly already gone mad.

Background: Loosely based on the real-life story of army radio dee-jay Adrian Cronauer, *Good Morning Vietnam* is as much a film about Robin Williams' comic ability as it is about the war in South East Asia. Indeed, the erstwhile comedian won an Oscar for Best Actor.

While the Second World War has often been ripe for comic films (*Kelly's Heroes* and *Stalag 17* being the two most obvious examples), Vietnam has rarely been a topic for humour. Films like *Air America* that have tried to use the conflict as a backdrop for comedy have been few and far between and have generally come unstuck at the box office. *Good Morning Vietnam*, however, succeeds because it is a film of two halves. Williams' opening monologues, reportedly improvised on set, are hilariously funny stand-up routines about Vietnam. In the second half of the film director Barry Levinson has the sense to punctuate the action that takes place outside of the radio station with enough of these monologues to keep the film afloat.

Although there's hardly a single mention of drugs in the film—other than Cronauer's quip "it's not a problem, everyone's got some"—*Good Morning Vietnam* deserves a place among the druggie/surreal 'Nam movies because it suggests (like *Apocalypse Now* and *Air America*) that America's involvement in the conflict was so insane that it verged on being absurd. The point is hammered home rather heavily by the montage of riots, fighting and firing squads set to the tune of Louis Armstrong's 'It's A Wonderful World'. In a war where stupidity and lunacy replace compassion and level-headedness, *Good Morning Vietnam* argues that Cronauer's blend of openness (his friendship with the local Vietnamese) and humour (his morale-boosting monologues) is the only true way of winning the populace's hearts and minds.

Air America (1990)

Crew: Director: Roger Spottiswoode. Producer: Daniel Melnick. Writers: Richard Rush, John Eskow, based on the novel by Christopher Robbins. Cinematographer: Roger Deakins. Editors: John Bloom, Lois Freeman-Fox.

Cast: Mel Gibson (Gene Ryack), Robert Downey Jr. (Billy Covington), Nancy Travis (Corine Landreaux), Ken Jenkins (Major Donald Lemond).

Summary: Laos, South East Asia, 1969. After losing his pilot's license in Los Angeles, fly boy Billy is recruited as part of the covert 'Air America' program in Laos. Run by the CIA, 'Air America' supplies humanitarian aid to anti-Communist forces across the border from Vietnam. Shocked by the craziness of his fellow pilots and by the fact that the American authorities are using money from the lucrative heroin trade to finance their operations, Billy tries to convince fellow pilot Gene to make a stand against the greed and corruption.

Subtext: As one of the CIA operatives explains to Billy, the war in Laos is supposedly different from the better-known conflict taking place across the border—"Vietnam is for niggers and no-necks; this is a gentleman's war." The film does everything it can to prove him wrong—the covert nature of the war in Laos is far from gentlemanly; rather, it's a symptom of American and Laotian greed where war aims are transplanted by the mechanics of business. The pilots' boast that they fly "Anything, Anywhere, Anytime" is less a proud fact of their bravery than the sign of their complete corruption (Gene's "retirement plan" involves gun-running).

Background: Like an update of *Catch-22* for the Vietnam era, *Air America* focuses on the insanity of war. Gibson's wisecracking pilot—"if he's not dead he's very, very calm"—is well aware of the surreal nature of the conflict; after all, unlike in Vietnam, there is officially no American presence in Laos—so, as Gene keeps pointing out, none of the terrible abuses that are happening are really "happening." The film's overriding message is "If you can't laugh at war, what's the point in fighting?" a sentiment that the liberal-focused sub-plot about saving refugees is supposed to counteract (but spectacularly fails to). Never as kooky or as politically subversive as it wants to be, Spottiswoode's ill-fated comedy fudges issues of the CIA's involvement in the South East Asia heroin trade, a theme that had already been touched on in an earlier and much better Mel Gibson movie, 1987's action classic *Lethal Weapon*. Rather than addressing the extent of the CIA's links with the opium growers, *Air America* settles back into broad farce. The Laotians are treated as greedy and vicious, believers in the get-rich-quick incentives of the American Dream who have no time for all that other crap about justice and liberty for all. There's an obligatory helicopter-suspended-in-a-tree scene (ripped off from *Apocalypse Now*) and some rather tired banter between the two stars. No wonder Downey Jnr. turned to drugs if this was the quality of the material he was being offered.

Jacob's Ladder (1990)

Crew: Director: Adrian Lyne. Producer: Alan Marshall. Writer: Bruce Joel Rubin. Cinematographer: Jeffrey Kimball. Editor: Tom Rolfe.

Cast: Tim Robbins (Jacob Singer), Elizabeth Pena (Jezebel), Matt Craven (Michael), Pruitt Taylor Vince (Paul), Danny Aiello (Louis).

Summary: After serving in Vietnam's Mekong Delta in 1971, Jacob Singer returns home to America (or does he?). Things seem fine but then he starts having visions of demons, his life seems to be threatened and there's a rumour that the army tested chemical weapons on his battalion. He keeps having flashbacks to Vietnam, but can't remember what happened on the night he was injured. Is he just suffering the delayed effects of some bad grass or is there something more sinister?

Subtext: Depends on how you want to look at the film. From a 'Nam perspective, Jacob's demonic visions are at once survivor's guilt (or post-traumatic stress) and also a result of the army's drug testing on unsuspecting grunts. But the story also works on different levels—a biblical tale of damnation and salvation; a story about war crimes; a story about a father's love for his dead son. The plot strands are so interwoven that each is integral to the next and you're left wondering if director Lyne is really the same man who made *Fatal Attraction*, *Flash-dance* and *9½ Weeks*.

Background: Marketed as a horror film rather than a Vietnam War film, *Jacob's Ladder* is actually neither—a hybrid horror/Vietnam/con-spiracy/melodrama that combines so many different genres that you're kept constantly on the edge of your seat. Merging the conventional vet movie with the kind of spooky atmospherics that are usually found in *The Twilight Zone*, *Jacob's Ladder* is a truly audacious entry in the Vietnam War film catalogue. As the legend that serves as the film's epi-logue highlights, the issue of drug testing on American soldiers by the military is supposedly based in fact. In the aftermath of the war there were several rumours about the military's use of hallucinogenic drugs on both the VC and American soldiers, although the Pentagon denied all of these accusations. Such rumours were frequent during the conflict and included the grunts' belief that the VC were spiking the various drugs that the infantry got hold off, as well as the equally plausible belief that the VC actively promoted the free flow of narcotics in order to weaken the American forces.

What makes *Jacob's Ladder* so memorable is the manner in which it uses these rumours about drug testing to greater ends. The film's hellish vision owes much to Hieronymous Bosch and (with reference to the fig-ures whose heads sway inhumanly fast from side to side) Francis Bacon's Screaming Pope pictures. But it's a vision that's closely tied to post-war guilt. The drug that the military tested on the grunts—dubbed 'the ladder' because it drops the user right into the bowels of their pri-mal fears—illustrates the fact that America's real enemy in Vietnam wasn't the VC (*Jacob's Ladder* is one of the few Vietnam films that doesn't include any VC in its flashback sequences) but America itself. The implicit suggestion is that the war was lost because of drugs and, more intriguingly, the military's failure to stem the flow of hallucino-gens in the field. Gives a whole new meaning to the phrase "war is hell."

5. "Hell No! We Won't Go!":

The Counter-culture & The Protest Movement

Although few people realized it at the time, Vietnam was a war fought on two fronts. While American troops where humping the boonies and taking fire in the jungles of South East Asia, a very different kind of war was happening back home. It was a war that emerged from the radical upheavals of the 1960s, from the civil rights demonstrations, from the hippie counter-culture and, of course, from the mind-blowing impact of lysergic acid diethylamide, or plain old LSD-25.

Because of its radicalism, the 1960s peace movement was never really part of Hollywood or the film-making process. Bob Hope and John Wayne were the reactionary stars who ruled the roost in the late 1960s—and their Hollywood had little time for the hippies or the peaceniks. As a result, there are very few films from the period about the peace protestors. A couple of films from what today we'd call left-field tapped into the Zeitgeist, but there were no real blockbusters and Hollywood didn't want to understand or even recognize the counter-culture until Jane Fonda's sudden and unexpected transformation into a peacenik forced Tinsel Town to sit up and pay attention.

A member of one of the most powerful Hollywood clans, Fonda was the least likely spokesperson for the counter-culture. Yet, in the upheaval of the late 1960s and early 1970s, she was transformed from pin-up girl (her *Barbarella* image) into one of the most hated women in America (dubbed 'Hanoi' Jane). At the height of her unpopularity, there was even a brisk trade in "Nuke Fonda" bumperstickers.

Fonda's reputation as a subversive rapidly grew throughout the late 1960s. At first her involvement with counter-cultural radicals—everyone from the peaceniks to the Black Panthers—was taken as a passing fad. But when she confirmed her status as Hollywood's most well-known drop-out hippie by visiting North Vietnam at the height of the war, her radical politics suddenly seemed more than just a joke and she was universally condemned by Hollywood's conservative elite when she took the opportunity to broadcast to American servicemen from

Hanoi: "I implore you, I beg you to consider what you are doing. All of you in the cockpits of your planes, on the aircraft carriers, those who are loading the bombs, those who are repairing the planes, those who are working on the Seventh Fleet, please think what you are doing. Are these people your enemy? What will you say to your children years from now when they ask you why you fought this war?"

For the North Vietnamese, it was as if all their Communist Christmases had come at once while in Washington, various senators demanded that Fonda be tried for treason (they were hampered by a technicality—since America had never officially declared war on North Vietnam, Fonda wasn't actually consorting with the enemy). Fonda's Vietnam visit caused a national scandal and thrust the peace protesters even further into the centre of the public's gaze. Needless to say, the documentary film about her travels through North Vietnam with husband Tom Hayden—entitled *Vietnam Journey*—didn't do much to improve her popularity rating among American conservatives.

While Fonda was showing how not to win friends and influence people (she was in the unenviable position of being hated by the establishment *and* by many of the protestors she wanted to help since they thought she couldn't be trusted), other members of the film industry were also trying to counter Hollywood's silence over the peace movement. Low-budget, independent films like *The Activist* caught the unruly spirit of the times and championed the political commitment of college students across America, while documentaries like *Hearts and Minds* (1974) became a prevalent part of the media landscape.

The Activist (1969)

Crew: Director: Art Napoleon. Producers: Art Napoleon, Jo Napoleon. Writers: Art Napoleon, Jo Napoleon. Cinematographer: Art Napoleon. Editor: Michael Kahn.

Cast: Michael Smith (Michael Corbett), Lesley Gilbrun (Lee James, 'Babe'), Tom Maier (Peter Williams), Benbow Ritchie (Home Owner).

Summary: Michael is a student activist who opposes the war in Vietnam and is involved in various subversive actions. Trying to shut down the city's local army induction centre, Michael and other demonstrators battle the police. Meanwhile, his girlfriend remembers their first meeting and recalls her changing interest in his politics—from ignorance to enthusiastic support to growing disenchantment. Michael's commitment to the attack on the induction centre inspires other activists to continue in the face of increasing police brutality even though his girlfriend, college professor and some of his fellow activists can't see the point anymore. The film ends as Michael goes off to join yet another attack on the centre.

Subtext: Michael supports his political radicalism by arguing "If I think something is wrong and I don't do anything about it, I don't exist." In such a context, Michael's activism becomes his literal *raison d'être* and the film explicitly suggests that his political commitment has superseded the imperatives of both romance and education (the advice he receives from his girlfriend and professor falls on deaf ears). Becoming a martyr—Michael links himself with Christ in his comment that he won't be happy until he has nails driven into his hands—obviously comes at a price.

Background: Capturing the spirit of the late 1960s, *The Activist* underlines the political radicalism that fuelled this turbulent period of civil unrest. Michael and the other student activists, many of whom were played by real-life demonstrators rather than actors, are idealists who refuse to compromise over their opposition of the war and suffer some very violent beatings as a result. Using actual footage from the period, the Napoleons' film creates a pseudo-documentary realism that—coupled with the fact that this indie film was made and released in 1969—gives it a veracity of action that no studio picture could ever hope to emulate. It's a shame, then, that's it's so rarely seen today.

Letter To Jane (1972)

Crew: Directors: Jean-Luc Godard, Jean-Pierre Gorin. Producers: Jean-Luc Godard, Jean-Pierre Gorin.

Voices: Jean-Luc Godard, Jean-Pierre Gorin.

Jean-Luc Godard's artistic involvement with Jane Fonda began in the early 1970s during the preproduction of *Tout Va Bien*. Desperate to find film stars who could guarantee this project some commercial appeal,

Godard cast Fonda and Yves Montand as the principal actors. Although Fonda was at the height of her reinvention as a left-wing radical, she was unconvinced by the project's politics and was browbeaten (in a three-hour, philosophical and political lecture from Jean-Pierre Gorin) into accepting the offer. Legend has it that *Letter To Jane* was something of a revenge attack on Fonda for being so reluctant to get involved with *Tout Va Bien*. But it was also, in the words of film writer Wheeler Winston Dixon, "a thoroughly brilliant but cruel examination of the iconics of Hollywood stardom."

This 53-minute film focuses on a single, still image of Jane Fonda that was taken while she was visiting Vietnam. The photograph, taken by Joseph Kraft, shows Fonda standing with a group of Vietnamese. Fonda is listening to one Vietnamese speaker whose face is obscured from the camera, so that the picture's main image is Fonda's serious face and slight bend of the head and back as she focuses her attention on the smaller, obscured and anonymous speaker. The photograph's original caption claims that the image shows Fonda *talking* to the Vietnamese (but, as Godard and Gorin point out, this is inaccurate. She's actually listening).

This image is the film's main picture. Godard and Gorin discuss the on-screen photograph and occasionally intercut it with images from *Klute*, *The Grapes Of Wrath*, *The Magnificent Ambersons* and publicity stills of Fonda from *Tout Va Bien*. The two French film-makers complain that Fonda's image is indicative of America's treatment of Asia. Her 'New Deal' expression is like that of her father in *The Grapes Of Wrath*—it's inherently condescending.

Godard and Gorin also claim that the American counter-culture (here represented by Fonda) is light years removed from the real revolutionaries of South East Asia. As a result, Fonda's well-meaning presence in Vietnam is just another form of American imperialism. Her Hollywood trappings mean that—as in the photograph—the world's attention is focused on Fonda the film star rather than the Vietnamese themselves. According to her French critics, she should say, as an American, "I'll keep my mouth shut because I admit I have nothing to say about this … I have to listen because I am not part of South East Asia."

While Godard and Gorin offer a very valid argument, their own paternalistic/patriarchal tone led some critics to suggest that their critique was somewhat misogynous. Fonda herself dismissed the film as "narrow-minded, male chauvinist sectarianism." Whatever the truth, *Letter To Jane* and the controversy that surrounded it highlighted the problematic relationship between fame and politics.

Hearts And Minds (1974)

Crew: Director: Peter Davis. Producers: Bert Schneider, Peter Davis. Cinematographer: Richard Pearce. Editors: Lynzee Klingman, Susan Martin.

In *Hearts And Minds*, documentary film maker Peter Davis tries to bring the war home to the majority of Americans whose only contact with the conflict had been through news reports and current affairs programmes. Focusing on the impact of the war on the Vietnamese themselves, Davis' blatant anti-war message is, in the words of one talking head, that "we aren't *on* the wrong side, we *are* the wrong side." Interviewing veterans, military commanders, Vietnamese civilians and even a former French president, *Hearts And Minds* tries to show that the war was wrong rather than mistaken—an ethical rather than a military failure.

Much of the film's impact comes from Davis' clever selection of material. In one celebrated sequence, the film juxtaposes scenes of Vietnamese civilians mourning the death of a family member with the comments of General Westmoreland, commander of the US forces in Vietnam, as he remarks that "the Oriental doesn't put the same value on human life as does the Westerner." The General's racist ideology is clearly exposed. Such predetermined judgement of the interviewees, however, is problematic. Davis' documentary so obviously categorizes its speakers in terms of being goodies or baddies that the audience is left wondering to what extent Davis' anti-war, anti-conservative beliefs are manipulating what we're being—or not being—shown. It's a brave film, but rather too partisan for its own good.

Coming Home (1978)

Crew: Director: Hal Ashby. Producer: Jerome Hellmann. Writers: Waldo Salt, Robert C Jones. Cinematographer: Haskell Wexler. Editor: Don Zimmerman.

Cast: Jane Fonda (Sally Hyde), Jon Voight (Luke Martin), Bruce Dern (Bob Hyde), Robert Carradine (Bill Munson).

Summary: When Captain Hyde takes a tour of duty in Vietnam his wife Sally volunteers to work at the local veterans' hospital where she's confronted with the realities of America's inadequate treatment of the returning wounded. In the hospital she meets Luke, an old high school friend who she slowly falls in love with. Visiting her husband in Hong Kong on R&R she realizes that they've drifted apart. Back in America she has an affair with Luke. Bob returns from the war suffering from post-traumatic stress and the government agents who've had Luke under surveillance because of his anti-war activism tell him about Sally's adultery. In a climatic confrontation he almost shoots the lovers but realizes that there's nothing he can do and so swims off into the sea.

Subtext: An explicitly anti-war film, *Coming Home* focuses not on the battlefield (there's not a single combat sequence) but on the domestic anti-war front. Contrasting the counter-culture (Luke's hippie style) against the military (Bob's starched uniforms), *Coming Home* gives the war a sexual dimension: Sally can't find sexual fulfilment with her husband whose energies are focused on the aggression that war requires and only the wheelchair-bound hippie protestor can offer her the "peace and love" that she requires.

Background: At the 1978 Oscar ceremony, *Coming Home* was in competition with a very different Vietnam War film, *The Deer Hunter*. While veterans protested outside (angry at *The Deer Hunter*'s portrayal of returning soldiers), Jane Fonda fuelled the controversy by declaring Cimino's film "a racist, Pentagon version of the war," and then later admitted that she hadn't seen the film. In the end, *The Deer Hunter* won Best Picture, with Voight and Fonda winning Best Actor and Actress for *Coming Home*. In retrospect, it's easy to see why the judges chose to give the Oscar to Cimino. For all its anti-war pretensions, *Coming Home* is really a sentimental romantic melodrama that uses Vietnam as a background for the burgeoning romance between Sally and Luke and the ultimate conflict with husband Voight. Sally's sexual/political transformation from good wife to independent woman (she changes her hair, gets a job, a new house, car and a new man while her husband's away) is more of a feminist statement that an anti-war protest, but *Coming Home* does at least manage to trace the links between war and facile machismo (Bob is decorated as a war hero even though he actually shot himself by accident on the way to the shower—quite emasculating) and men's fear of women's sexuality (raging against his adulterous wife Bob confusedly calls her a "slope cunt," thereby conflating the VC with the hippie/feminist uprising at home)

Yet, for all its sentimental faults, *Coming Home* was the first mainstream movie to recognize that Vietnam was a war fought on two fronts—one in South East Asia and one at home between vets, civilians, counter-cultural protestors and the silent majority. It may not know exactly what it's supposed to do with this domestic conflict, but at least it manages to recognize that it exists, while in the process giving Fonda's reinvention into a peacenik the blockbuster stamp of approval.

Running On Empty (1988)

Crew: Director: Sidney Lumet. Producers: Amy Robinson, Griffin Dunne. Writer: Naomi Foner. Cinematographer: Gerry Fisher. Editor: Andrew Mondshein.

Cast: Christine Lahti (Annie Pope), River Phoenix (Danny Pope), Judd Hirsch (Arthur Pope), Martha Plimpton (Lorna Phillips)

Summary: Annie and Arthur Pope are Sixties radicals who are still being hunted by the FBI in the 1980s for blowing up a napalm factory during the Vietnam War. Moving from town to town, they try and stay one step ahead of 'the Man'. Their two children are suffering the consequences of their outlaw lifestyle, though—particularly 17-year-old Danny who wants to go to college but knows that that would mean leaving his parents.

Subtext: Sidney Lumet's sensitive and engrossing film explores the impact of political commitment on the individuals involved. As a result of the Popes' anti-war statement, several lives have been ruined—a janitor was wounded in the blast, Arthur and Annie's parents have been abandoned, their children have been denied a 'normal' childhood and the hippie couple themselves have been condemned to a life of wandering.

Background: While draft dodgers eventually received government amnesty, the actions of counter-cultural radicals weren't so readily dismissed. Although the Popes are completely opposed to the violent revolution espoused by the anarchist hippies known as the Weathermen (one of whom wants them to help him rob a bank), they still have to wrestle with the moral consequences of their teenage actions. Lives have been ruined because of their opposition to the war in Vietnam—does that mean that they were wrong?

Sidney Lumet's intelligent drama doesn't have answers to such questions. Instead, the film offers an image of rehabilitation as Danny leaves the family in order to study music at college. By acknowledging their eldest son's needs and ultimately encouraging him to return to normal society, the Popes show that even though their lives have been irrevocably changed because of the bombing there is hope for the next generation—a generation that will have hopefully learnt from the mistakes of both hawks and doves in the past. It's only through realizing that their son shouldn't be made "to carry the burden of someone else's life" that the Popes are able to justify their continuing flight from the law.

Rude Awakening (1989)

Crew: Director: Aaron Russo, David Greenwalt. Producer: Aaron Russo. Writers: Neil Levy, Richard LaGravenese. Cinematographer: Tim Siegel. Editor: Paul Fried.

Cast: Cheech Martin (Jesus), Eric Roberts (Fred), Robert Carradine (Sammy), Buck Henry (Lloyd Stool), Louise Lasser (Bonnie).

Summary: In the 1960s, Fred and Jesus are radical hippie activists who are being chased by the Justice Department for dodging the draft and generally being subversive. Escaping to Central America they found a commune and live a life full of free love and grass-smoking. Things change in 1989 when they stumble over CIA plans outlining an imminent US invasion. Returning to the States to leak the story, they find that the world they left behind has gone and everyone has sold out to capitalism. Appalled they try and reawaken the populace's consciousness.

Subtext: Rude Awakening suggests that its hippie heroes have sold out just as much as their Reaganite, yuppie counterparts by hiding away in the jungles of Central America smoking pot for two decades. Instead of changing the world, Fred and Jesus have simply retreated from it. The worrying suggestion in *Rude Awakening* is that the ills of the 1980s (from acid rain to crack cocaine) are a result of the counter-culture's selling-out, although by its conclusion the film does suggest that these aging stoners will be able to redeem themselves by becoming politically committed again.

Background: Although there's little overt mention of the Vietnam War, *Rude Awakening* is shaped by the conflict. The two heroes (all Cheech and no Chong) escape America to avoid the draft and return home twenty years later because they want to stop an American invasion of South America that's just as stupid and morally wrong as Vietnam. It's really a one-joke fish-out-of-water movie (maybe that's the symbolic point of the stoned fish who keeps popping up in unlikely places?) in which the hippies have to confront 1980s apathy, greed and—horror of horrors—the colorisation of black and white movies. But what's interesting is the film's belief that if faced with another Vietnam, the American public would make the same mistakes as they did before—the Central American invasion (that was actually only a war game until the hippies leaked the story and favourable public opinion encouraged the President to go really to war) is greeted with an enthusiastic reinstatement of the draft. Clearly America has learnt nothing from Vietnam and parallels with contemporary incursions into foreign territory (Panama, Nicaragua and Grenada) seem blindingly obvious. Considering the film's release at the end of the 1980s it's tempting to read this second-rate comedy as a sign of the times—after all, the 1990s are often said to have been a reworking of the 1960s. Perhaps *Rude Awakening* prefigures the 1990s obsession with eradicating the political, social and ethical mistakes of the 1980s.

Crew: Director: Nancy Savoca. Producers: Richard Guay, Peter Newman. Writer: Bob Comfort. Cinematographer: Bobby Bukowski. Editor: John Tintori.

Cast: River Phoenix (Eddie Birdlace), Lili Taylor (Rose), Richard Panebianco (Bergin), Anthony Clark (Buele), Mitchell Whitfield (Benjamin).

Summary: November 1963. Four young marines are enjoying their last night of freedom before being shipped off to Vietnam where they're going to advise the local army on fighting the Communist insurgents. Each soldier has to find an ugly date to take to a 'dogfight' contest. The man with the ugliest girl wins the $100 pot. Birdlace picks up a shy folk-singing waitress in the Haight-Ashbury district of San Francisco and takes her along, but slowly falls in love with her. After she finds out about the contest he takes her out on a proper date and they spend the night together. In the late 1960s, after several tours in Vietnam, he comes back to look for her.

Subtext: Through a combination of artistic license and liberal idealism, the film takes place on the night before President Kennedy's assassination on 22 November 1963. As Birdlace is shipped out to Vietnam America's golden age and its innocent idealism crumble in Dallas, Texas. The assassination gets only a few seconds of screen time, but it's clear that director Savoca wants us to understand the war as part of a national fall from grace that follows JFK's death.

Background: Dogfight is a film in three sections. The first, longest section takes place on the night before Phoenix and his buddies ship out. The peacenik folk-singer confronts the macho, foul-mouthed (and yet so naïve) Marine. She challenges his bravado and, on discovering the truth about the dance contest, gives him a reality check: "you're a cruel, heartless ignorant creep and if I were a man I'd beat you to a pulp." She spends the rest of the evening trying to make him see through the army's brainwashing in the hope of getting him to view the world from her liberal perspective. Sadly, she fails—in the second act he ships off to Vietnam, doesn't write her, gets blown up and then, in the third act, comes home to find Haight-Ashbury transformed into hippie central ("How many babies you kill?" asks one of the long-haired passers-by). The film's take on the action is blatantly obvious—its feminist, pro-peace sentiments are truly rammed down the viewer's throat with the subtlety of a marine corps drill instructor. Savoca offers a fairly romanticized portrait of 1960s San Francisco that just seems a little too artificial to convince. But what saves *Dogfight* from degenerating into a facile piece of liberal sermonizing are the excellent performances from the two leads. Phoenix does a good job at capturing the fragile bravado of the raw recruit, but it's Taylor's movie—her deft characterisation of a pretty unbelievable character (Rose is so saintly it's sickening) saves the film and through her, *Dogfight* almost achieves a poignancy that the rest of its sledgehammer posturing could only dream of.

Forrest Gump (1994)

Crew: Director: Robert Zemeckis. Producers: Wendy Finerman, Steve Tisch, Steve Starkey. Writer: Eric Roth. Cinematographer: Don Burgess. Editor: Arthur Schmidt.

Cast: Tom Hanks (Forrest Gump), Robin Wright (Jenny Curran), Gary Sinise (Lieutenant Dan Taylor), Mykelti Williamson ('Bubba' Bufford-Blue), Sally Field (Mrs Gump).

Summary: The ever so slightly backward Forrest Gump tells his life story, including his experiences in Vietnam and his love for his girl-friend Jenny, who gets involved with Sixties counter-culture. Meeting a variety of famous Americans—from JFK to Nixon—Gump is acciden-tally embroiled in some of history's great moments but is never aware enough to realize the importance of the events he witnesses. Jenny, meanwhile, finds that the rebellious lifestyle she adopts actually brings nothing but unhappiness and dies wishing that she'd stayed with stupid but kind Forrest.

Subtext: For all its liberal posturing, *Forrest Gump* is undoubtedly one of the most insidious reactionary films to have come out of 1990s Hollywood. Its unacknowledged subtext (and the reason for the film's inclusion in this chapter) is its depiction of 1960s counter-culture as a childish, stupid and plain dangerous social phenomenon. While much is made of Forrest's military service during the Vietnam War where he

73

wins the Congressional Medal of Honor for his heroic rescue of his platoon, the main focus of the film's Vietnam section is the contrast of the experiences of Gump (stupid but heroic serviceman) and Jenny (stupid and selfish hippie).

Background: Winner of several Oscars, *Forrest Gump*'s central message is that ignorance is bliss and stupidity is the best policy. Forrest excels in the army ("I fit in the army like one of those round pegs") simply because he isn't clever enough to think for himself. He's so stoopid that, in his own words, Vietnam was good fun because: "I got to see lots of the countryside ... we'd take these real long walks and we were always looking for this guy named Charlie." The war is shown on both fronts—South East Asia and domestic—but the counter-culture (from peacenicks to the SDS to the Black Panthers) is supposedly comprised of women-beating cowards who put their self-interest over and above the national interest (fighting and winning the Vietnam War). Forrest's admission "I don't know much about anything" is applauded rather than treated as a character defect and the film's ideological message is that stay-at-home and do-as-you're-told conservatism is far better than having anything to do with the licentious peacenik-Beatnik-hippie counter-culture that, according to the film's revisionist history lesson, was directly responsible for the heroin-, crack- and AIDS-ravaged Eighties. *Forrest Gump* is Hollywood at its most horrendous, restyling the counter-culture of the 1960s and the anti-war protest movement as a cultural blip rather than a progressive social movement that fought to end the war, promote civil rights and challenge conservatism run amok. What's most worrying of all is that the British Board of Film Classification saw fit to give this evil little film a U certificate. How can we protect our children against such insidious brainwashing?

6. "Do We Get To Win This Time?":
The 1980s Return To 'Nam

Under Ronald Reagan's presidency, America finally began to emerge from the hangover of Vietnam. With a cowboy president in the White House, Vietnam became the war that should have been won, a mistake that the Reagan administration vocally admitted to (on behalf of former presidents) and assured the public it would never repeat again. Reinterpreting the war in this way allowed Reagan to reinterpret America's status as a world power. At a time when Grenada, the Middle East, the Evil Empire of the Soviet Union were foreign policy hot spots and America was styled as the crusading force of power and justice. Reagan made his post-Vietnam military strategy perfectly clear. As war in the Middle East seemed an increasingly likely possibility, Reagan quipped: "Boy, I saw *Rambo* last night; now I know what to do next time."

In keeping with the can-do optimism of the Reagan years, Hollywood had begun to reassess the Vietnam War. In place of the 'war is hell' combat movies, melodramatic veterans sagas or weepy protest films that had been established in the years since 1978, Hollywood created a new subgenre, the gung-ho, reactionary wish-fulfilment replay of the Vietnam War. Unlike the metaphorical replays of Vietnam found in *Deliverance* or *Southern Comfort*, this cycle of films sent American forces back 'in country' to finish the job that the bureaucrats (and it is almost always the paper-pushing chair warmers who are branded responsible) had stopped the troops from finishing in the 1970s.

As subgenres go, the 'Return to 'Nam' cycle was fairly low-budget. With the exception of the subgenre's most famous son, *Rambo. First Blood Part II*, most of the films about the search for American prisoners of war on Vietnamese soil were cheap and cheerful action fests, often with a B or C list movie star like Chuck Norris. What they offered, though, in spite of the shoddy production values, was the chance, in Rambo's words, "to win this time."

Not everyone was convinced with these films' politics. Not only did they fuel speculation that there were still prisoners of war (POWs) held in Vietnam (a belief that must have given many families of missing servicemen false hope), but they encouraged the kind of knee-jerk, imperialist racism that most critics found hard to stomach. Many former servicemen were opposed to the films' simplification of the issues and when *Rambo* opened in Boston, veterans picketed the cinemas with placards reading "Reality Not Rambo." Re-imagining the war in such crude, jingoistic terms was not only politically suspect, but it also deflected attention from the social problems that veterans still faced.

The 'Return to 'Nam' cycle did have one positive influence, though. It paved the way for the reworking of the combat film that occurred in the later part of the 1980s. Films like *Platoon, Hamburger Hill* and *Full Metal Jacket*, with their emphasis on authenticity, were, in part, reactions against the oversimplification of the Vietnam conflict that the *Rambo* cycle had encouraged.

Good Guys Wear Black (1977)

Crew: Director: Ted Post. Producer: Alan F Bodoh. Writers: Joseph Fraley, Bruce Cohn, Mark Medoff. Cinematographer: Robert Steadman. Editors: William Moore, Millie Moore.

Cast: Chuck Norris (John T Booker), Anne Archer (Margaret), Lloyd Haynes (Murray Saunders), Dana Andrews (Edgar J Harolds).

Summary: During the Paris peace talks in the final days of the war, a group of CIA operatives are sent into Vietnam in search of proof of MIA/POWs being held by the VC. But the mission is a failure. Five years later, Booker discovers the truth about the conspiracy. Meanwhile, someone is assassinating the surviving members of his team. Booker pieces the complex plot together and realizes that it was the politician at the Paris peace talks who sacrificed the CIA team to win favour with the Vietnamese negotiators.

Subtext: Clearly taking place in the shadow of Watergate's political corruption, *Good Guys Wear Black* is a deeply sceptical film that suggests that Booker's betrayal in Vietnam is indicative of the experience of every soldier who fought in the war. The venal politicians in Washington sold all of them out under the guise of expediency.

Background: The first of Chuck Norris' Vietnam action films contains surprisingly little action. Ted Post (the man who would go on to direct *Go Tell The Spartans*) doesn't seem to realize that Norris can't act. Instead of making this an action showcase for Norris' martial arts abilities he tries to craft a convoluted conspiracy thriller instead— hardly an approach that Norris' CV would recommend. The result is one of the most boring action star vehicles ever made, with an opening battle scene that's so badly lit it's impossible to tell what's happening and a ludicrously complex plot that's virtually impossible to follow. The film's only significance is that it initiates the 'we were sold out by Washington' motif that runs throughout most of the 'Return to 'Nam' films. In his final confrontation with the corrupt senator, Norris warns "if you get away with this it will betray every guy who died in any war" and then proceeds to drown the dirty politico in the ocean—a clear example of water-as-purification symbolism if ever there was one. Fortunately for the box-office receipts, the rest of the films in this subgenre ditched the complex plots in favour of more lurid action sequences.

Uncommon Valor (1983)

Crew: Director: Ted Kotcheff. Producers: John Milius, Buzz Feitshans. Writer: Joe Gayton. Cinematographer: Stephen H Burum. Editor: Mark Melnick.

Cast: Gene Hackman (Colonel Rhodes), Robert Stack (MacGregor), Fred Ward (Wilkes), Randall 'Tex' Cobb (Sailor), Patrick Swayze (Kevin Scott).

Summary: Convinced that his son is still being held in a Vietnamese POW camp, Rhodes regroups the surviving members of his son's platoon and organizes a mission to free the remaining American POWs. After a lengthy training sequence, the vets head out to South East Asia. The American government impounds their equipment and they're forced to complete the mission using second-hand weapons. Although several of the team are killed in the fighting and Rhodes discovers that

77

his son died while in the camp, the mission is successful and Rhodes returns with a group of American POWs.

Subtext: As the Korean War veteran ready to put his life on the line to bring the remaining American boys in Vietnam, Rhodes is a potent symbol of the good patriarch who, in contrast to the Washington bureaucrats who claim their hands are tied by diplomatic constraints, is unwilling to let the war end until the MIA/POW issue has been resolved. Organizing the mission with a messianic fervour and exploiting the guilty consciences of each of the veterans he recruits, Rhodes is justice/revenge personified. As he himself claims, "This time no one can dispute the rightness of what we're doing."

Background: An unexpected sleeper hit, *Uncommon Valor* singlehandedly kick-started the 'Return to 'Nam' subgenre with its combination of action and moral self-righteousness. Directed and produced by the same team responsible for *First Blood* (Kotcheff and Feitshans), with a co-producer credit for John Milius (who had a hand in *Apocalypse Now* and several other Vietnam films), *Uncommon Valor* is a cut above most of the 'Return to 'Nam' films that it inspired. Its cast includes several name actors (Ward, Swayze and, of course, Gene Hackman) as well as cult actor 'Tex' Cobb.

Commenting on the 'unfinished business' of the war, Rhodes reminds his assembled mercenaries about the short shrift that they received from the US government: "You cost too much and didn't turn a profit." But not only did the US government stop the soldiers from winning the war they also meddled so much that—according to *Uncommon Valor*'s scriptwriter, at least—the war was left incomplete, with American servicemen trapped in POW camps for over a decade. Such focus on the MIA/POW issue serves a cathartic function, letting the audience realize that the war was lost yet also giving one last opportunity for American forces to prove that they deserved to win. Much like *First Blood*, the action set pieces culminate in a surprising scene of grief—the climatic battle ends with Rhodes weeping for the loss of his son. But as the epilogue in which he's reunited with his wife (who's been pointedly forced to stay at home throughout the film) shows, after grief comes redemption—a message that was obviously meant to extend to America itself.

Crew: Director: Joseph Zito. Producers: Menahem Golan, Yoram Globus. Writer: James Bruner. Cinematographer: Joao Fernand. Editors: Joel Goodman, Daniel Lowenthal.

Cast: Chuck Norris (Colonel James Braddock), M Emmet Walsh (Tuck), David Tress (Senator Porter), Leonore Kasdorf (Ann).

Summary: Vietnam veteran Colonel Braddock becomes involved in the search for American MIA soldiers. A loose cannon, Braddock takes matters into his own hands, teaming up with an old comrade in arms, Tuck, to rescue the prisoners. Returning to Vietnam, they are pursued by Vietnamese agents but manage to locate and free four American prisoners. Tuck is killed helping the others escape. Braddock returns to confront the American and Vietnamese politicians with the proof that MIAs are still alive in Vietnam.

Subtext: Deliberately setting itself up as a comic book wish-fulfilment fantasy—Braddock even watches a *Spiderman* cartoon on television—*Missing In Action* is a violent, racist action film that has as much to do with 1980s politics as the spectre of Vietnam. In one scene, Braddock bizarrely sees a woman in Middle Eastern garb in Thailand suggesting that this fantasy of American heroism and gun-barrel justice has a contemporary point to make about the Free World's post-Vietnam enemies.

Background: Clearly conceived as a vehicle for Chuck Norris' action (but limited acting) talents, *Missing In Action* actually came to possess a deeper resonance as a filmic parallel of Ronald Reagan's tough-guy infatuation with the MIA/POW issue. In typical subgenre fashion, *Missing In Action* allows Braddock to replay the Vietnam War—and win. Ignoring the two-faced Washington bureaucrats, Braddock brings home living proof that there are still American servicemen being held in Vietnam and arrives back in Ho Chi Minh City just as the American and Vietnamese politicians have concluded that no such prisoners exist. Braddock's all-American gung-ho self-reliance proves that the gooks are dirty liars and, more importantly, that the Washington pen-pushers are pusillanimous cowards.

With its truly awful production values, *Missing In Action* should have sunk without trace into the dark depths of mid-1980s exploitation cinema, but its politics were popular enough to ensure a healthy life on the video shop shelves and (quite unbelievably) two sequels—the 1985 *Missing In Action 2: The Beginning* and the 1988 *Braddock: Missing In Action 3*. Each of these truly dismal wastes of celluloid make the *Rambo* cycle look like *Citizen Kane*.

Rambo: First Blood Part II (1985)

Crew: Director: George P Cosmatos. Producer: Buzz Feitshans. Writers: Sylvester Stallone, James Cameron. Cinematographer: Jack Cardiff. Editors: Mark Goldblatt, Mark Helfirch, Gib Jaffe, Frank E Jiminez, Larry Block.

Cast: Sylvester Stallone (John Rambo), Richard Crenna (Colonel Trautman), Julia Nickson-Soul (Co Bao), Charles Napier (Murdock), Steven Berkoff (Lt. Colonel Podovsky), Martin Kove (Ericson).

Summary: John Rambo is released from prison to lead a recon mission deep in the heart of Vietnam in search of American POWs. After a disastrous parachute jump, Rambo meets his contact, a Vietnamese woman, and finds the camp and the prisoners. But the special operation's leader, Murdock, betrays him in order to cover up the fact that American POWs are still being held in Vietnam. After single-handedly battling the VC and their Russian allies, Rambo leads the POWs safely home.

Subtext: Rambo is a comic book wish-fulfilment fantasy without equal. The script is crude enough about its replay of the war that even the dumbest viewer could understand its intent; as he accepts the mission Rambo pointedly asks his former commander: "Sir? Do we get to win this time?" The rest of the film leaves you in no doubt that this time the answer is a definite yes.

The Background: Criticized for its ultra-violent action and its reactionary treatment of the POW issue, *Rambo First Blood Part II* is best considered pure popcorn entertainment. It lacks the psychological depth that made *First Blood* such a surprisingly effective film, focusing instead of the transformation of Rambo into a mythical fighting machine devoid of brains, wit or intelligence whose only desire is "to win a war that someone else lost." It's hard to imagine anything more conservative than Stallone and James Cameron's screenplay. The burden of guilt for the loss of Vietnam is placed squarely on Washington bureaucrats' shoulders—according to the film, the political decision not to pay war reparations to the VC in 1972 forestalled the release of the POWs and encouraged rearguard seat warmers like Murdock (whose own combat experience is a fiction) to bury the whole issue. Rambo is double-crossed by his own colleagues in an oh-so-obvious repeat of the betrayal of Vietnam veterans by America itself. The film's racial politics are also suspect—an actress who's probably the most western-looking girl in the whole of South East Asia plays Rambo's Vietnamese love interest. What's more, the film offers an anti-Russian sub-plot that's an entrée for Stallone's return in *Rambo III* in which he single-handedly wins the Cold War, fighting those dratted Russkies in Afghanistan. Like the majority of action films *Rambo* trades on a masochistic kind of pleasure. Eighty percent of the film involve watching our muscled hero get shot, cut, tortured, suspended in pig shit and electrified. The other twenty percent see him take his revenge. You've got to wonder, what kind of pleasure does the (predominantly male) audience get from watching Rambo's ultra-masculine body get so abused?

Probably the most well known film in the 'Return to 'Nam' sub-genre, *Rambo* is an orgy of comic book violence that believes that "to survive a war you've gotta become war." Nice.

Eye Of The Eagle (1987)

Crew: Director: Cirio H Santiago. Producer: Cirio H Santiago. Writer: Joseph Zucchero. Cinematographer: Ricardo Remias. Editor: Gervacio Santos.

Cast: Brett Clark (Sergeant Rick Stratton), Robert Patrick (Corporal Johnny Ransom), Ed Crick (Sergeant Rattner), William Steis (Captain Carter).

Summary: When a group of GI deserters and MIAs go on the rampage in the jungles of Vietnam, the top brass call in a crack squad of assassins code-named 'Eagle'. Comprised of Ransom, Carter and a

South Vietnamese special forces operative, the Eagle team have a score to settle with the so-called 'Lost Command' since the leader of this renegade band killed Rick's brother. If this synopsis makes the film sound halfway coherent, forget it—*Eye Of The Eagle*'s plot is a ridiculous mess.

Subtext: What are you kidding? The film barely knows what the main text is!

Background: This incompetent, truly atrocious film is the nadir of the mid-1980s 'Nam films. Although it's set during the war (rather than returning to the war at a later date), it deserves to be placed alongside *Rambo: First Blood Part II*, *Missing In Action* and their various imitators solely because of its overblown comic book style and its politics (although it must be said that it's such amateurish nonsense that it only really deserves to be burnt to a crisp). The photography is terrible, the sets are ludicrous (a hospital 'set' contains nothing more than a white-washed wall, a Give Blood poster and a bed with an IV drip), the dialogue is ridiculous, the continuity is all over the place and the acting is some of the worst ever committed to celluloid. In terms of bad film-making, this makes Ed Wood's *Plan 9 From Outer Space* look like *The Seventh Seal*.

For what it's worth, *Eye Of The Eagle* trots out most of the ideological nonsense associated with the 'Return to 'Nam' subgenre. Characters comment (rather woodenly) on the fact that the war is futile because the bureaucrats won't let the American forces win—and the renegade soldiers of The Lost Command are vaguely sympathized with because their disgruntled refusal to continue fighting for Uncle Sam is understandable given the usual 'we're being betrayed by Washington' mentality. However, the Eagle team don't waste any time in killing the renegades off in order to preserve military law and order.

The Western influences that we've seen in other films are paid ludicrous a homage—one of the Eagle team carries an old-fashioned six-shooter and (I'm not making this up) a Winchester rifle. The only interesting thing about this utter debacle is the fact that it stars Robert Patrick, the man who would later play Arnie's nemesis in *Terminator 2*. Presumably he didn't mention his starring role in this Z-movie to the casting director.

7. "When Heaven & Earth Collided":
Telling A Different Story

While Hollywood films about Vietnam inevitably dominated cinemas, there were also other films about the conflict. The most obvious source of such films is Vietnam itself, where the fight against the US forces was known as "the American War." But, it's indicative of just how one-sided our western view of the conflict is that films from South East Asia that deal with the war are hardly ever seen in Europe or America.

According to Phan Dinh Mau's 1992 essay 'The War And Vietnamese Films', there are two moments in post-1970 Vietnamese cinema. Up until 1975, North Vietnam focused on making propaganda combat films that were designed to instil audiences with a sense of patriotic duty. After 1975, as North and South were reunited, a more reflective style of film-making emerged that sought to examine the aftermath of war and the gradual return of peace.

Searching the video libraries, rental shops and record stores for VHS or DVD copies of the thousands of Vietnamese films that have been released during and after the war is a depressing experience. Occasionally a mainstream gem of Vietnamese cinema, like Tran Anh Hung's *Cyclo*, will make it into our cinemas or, if we're less lucky, into the graveyard shift TV schedules, but for the most part, films that deal explicitly with the American War like *White Flowers On The River* (*Dong Song Hoa Trang*, 1989) or *Fairy Tale For Seventeen Year Olds* (*Truyen Co Tich Cho Tuoi 17*, 1987) are impossible to find. Jean-Jacques Malo and Tony Williams' encyclopaedia of Vietnam War films lists around 137 features produced by Vietnam's national cinema industry, yet only one or two of these have ever made it over here.

America may have lost the ground war in Vietnam, but it won the cultural battle for domination of the world's cinema screens with its stories of veterans, gunfights and POWs. But then again, Vietnam isn't the only cinema that has produced films about the war. Countries as far removed as Australia, France and Hong Kong have all contributed to the international body of films about the Vietnam War. This chapter focuses on a few of these films—giving preference to the ones that are most likely to be found on video or on television—as well as discussing America's only attempt to offer a Vietnamese perspective on the war, Oliver Stone's *Heaven & Earth*.

Heroes Shed No Tears (Ying Xiong Wei Lei) (1986)

Crew: Director: John Woo. Producer: Peter Chan. Writer: John Woo. Cinematographer: Naragawa Kenichi. Editor: Chang Yiu Chung.

Cast: Eddy Ko Hung (Chan Chung), Lam Ching-Ying (Vietnamese Colonel), Chen Yue-Sang (Ching yut Sang), Lau Chau-Sang (Chau Sang).

Summary: A group of Chinese mercenaries is hired by the Thai government to capture a Vietnamese general who's running the South East Asia drug trade. The mission goes to plan, but the Vietnamese army chases the mercenaries. Teaming up with an American veteran from the Vietnam War, they fight a pitched battle against their pursuers before escaping to freedom.

Subtext: The moral of this noisy slice of Heroic Bloodshed cinema is that the wages of greed are death. All the money-grabbing characters—from the evil drug baron general to the gamblers in the mercenary unit—are taught not to hanker after gold, silver or U.S. dollars. One of the good guys finds that his avarice results in a rather nasty death-by-dismemberment.

Background: A precursor of *Bullet In The Head*, *Heroes Shed No Tears* is John Woo's take on the kind of 'Return to 'Nam' subgenre that was dominating the American markets in the mid-1980s although, significantly, the film lacks the sledgehammer politics that characterized movies like *Uncommon Valor* and *Rambo: First Blood Part II*. *Heroes Shed No Tears* is only really interested in the Vietnam War as a backdrop for several kinetic action sequences which, although lacking the now clichéd 'balletic' grace of Woo's later films, are violent enough to keep most war film junkies happy. There's also plenty of unintentionally hilarious subtitling (the print I saw contained numerous gaffes and non sequiturs in the on-screen translations—"Anything the matter?" asks one character as his friend gets knocked off his feet by gunfire.)

Woo's fascination with guns and bullets and, in particular, rounds being chambered, suggests a full-blown fetishism with the art of shooting, while at least one scene makes a brief blink-and-you'll-miss-it allusion to *The Deer Hunter* as gambler Ching has a gun pointed at his head he asks if his assailants want to play Russian Roulette. There's a half-baked subplot about the Chinese mercenaries wanting to escape to America (the Thai government has promised them green cards in exchange for the general) and this, coupled with the appearance of a conventionally crazy American Vietnam veteran—his first scene finds him wired to a mound of explosives—who's abandoned his homeland in favour of a paradise of dope smoking and Vietnamese peasant girls suggests that Woo's screenplay is trying to say something about the need for Chinese nationals to be wary of being seduced away to the West. The American vet warns his Chinese friend that America is just as much of "a dog-eat-dog society." All this introspection is, of course, quickly shattered by gunfire and the insistent thud of several hundred dead bodies hitting the floor which is, after all, the whole point of a Hong Kong action film. The broader, more ambitious, canvas of *Bullet In The Head* was still a few years away in Woo's filmography.

Dear America: Letters Home From Vietnam (1987)

Crew: Director: Bill Couturie. Producers: Bill Couturie, Thomas Bird. Writer: Richard Dewhurst, Bill Couturie. Cinematographer: Michael Chin. Editors: Stephen Stept, Gary Weinberg.

Produced by American cable channel HBO, this film adaptation of a book of collected GI letters was designed by director Bill Couturie as "a scrapbook, a time capsule." Newsreel footage, home movies and material from the Department of Defense archives are used as background to the narration of various letters home from GIs to their families. Read by actors like Robert De Niro, Martin Sheen and Tom Berenger, Ellen Burstyn and Kathleen Turner, the letters are supposed to offer a first-hand portrait of the war, told by those who were actually there. In the words of the director, "the idea is to let multiple sets of voices speak for themselves, with my own author's voice muted and marginalized as commentary."

However, as more than once critic has noted, many of the letters have been edited for the film, with certain, politically sensitive, comments excised. For all Couturie's attempts to style the film as politically neutral, it does seem that *Dear America*'s attempts to avoid controversy by ignoring (or actively editing out) the 'difficult' issues surrounding the war allies this film with a conservative policy of hear-no-evil, see-no-evil, speak-no-evil avoidance.

Bullet In The Head (Diexue Jietou) (1990)

Crew: Director: John Woo. Producer: John Woo. Writer: John Woo, Patrick Leung, Janet Chun. Cinematographers: Ardy Lam, Wilson Chan, Somcahi Kittikun, Wong Wing-Hang. Editor: John Woo.

Cast: Tony Leung (Ben), Jacky Cheung (Frank), Waise Lee (Paul), Simon Yam (Luke).

Summary: Three friends (Ben, Paul and Frank) leave Hong Kong in 1967 to seek their fortune working in Vietnam's black market. Falling foul of a local mobster they steal his gold and his girl and head out into the countryside with the help of a fellow Hong Kong national, Luke. Captured by the VC the three friends are tortured until Luke and the Americans arrive to rescue them. Paul becomes obsessed with the gold, shooting Frank in the head and escaping along the river. Later, Ben and Luke find Frank—now a psychotic junkie with Paul's bullet lodged in his brain—in Saigon. After Frank dies, Ben swears revenge and battles Paul in a climatic gunfight.

Subtext: Greed is very definitely bad—it's the film's only theme and we're never allowed to forget it. The Hong Kong mobsters advise the eager young boys to go to Saigon since "cash follows chaos every time"; Paul abandons all his friends for a case full of gold and believes that guns can get you anything you want, as long as you're willing to ruthlessly pull the trigger.

Background: Picking up the themes of *Heroes Shed No Tears*, but with a far more mature approach, *Bullet In The Head* is an epic morality play. John Woo's film takes in the Hong Kong independence riots of the late 1960s, the underworld of Saigon (styled as some 1960s *Casablanca*, complete with friendly piano player), the VC, the American forces and Buddhist monks. Woo makes explicit references to *The Deer Hunter*, particularly in the POW camp scenes (where the characters are forced to shoot their fellow prisoners) and in his treatment of Frank's destitute state (like Nick, Frank becomes a drug-addicted zombie). But Woo's film is far more explosive than Cimino's studied drama with hundreds of shoot-outs, fights and even helicopter attacks. The title explicitly refers to Frank's unfortunate betrayal by his friend—but Woo hammers home its wider significance with a relentless series of images of headshots, most notably the execution of a VC suspect that bears a striking resemblance to Eddie Adam's famous news photograph. Woo compares the madness of Vietnam to having a bullet in the head Whether the significance of such a simple message survives the two-hour onslaught of chaos that Woo serves up is a moot point.

Turtle Beach (1992)

Crew: Director: Stephen Wallace. Producer: Matt Carroll. Writer: Ann Turner, based on the novel by Blanche d'Alpuget. Cinematographer: Russell Boyd. Editor: Lee Smith.

Cast: Greta Scacchi (Judith), Joan Chen (Minou), Jack Thompson (Ralph), Art Malik (Kanan), Norman Kaye (Hobday)

Summary: Australian journalist Judith travels to Malaysia to investigate the story of the Vietnamese refugees ("boat people") who are fleeing Communist Vietnam. She meets a Vietnamese ex-prostitute Minou and an Indian black marketer, Kanan, who show her Turtle Beach, where the Vietnamese land. Trying not to become embroiled in the political problems surrounding the refugees, Judith discovers that Minou is waiting for her children to arrive from Vietnam. But as the boat carrying them arrives, the local Malaysians threaten to kill the refugees and Minou has to sacrifice herself to scare them away.

Subtext: The Vietnamese boat people are the "Jews of Asia" and are being herded into modern-day concentration camps. Landing on Turtle Beach—the last breeding ground for the giant green turtle—the refugees only want to start a new life (follow the symbolism?). But the

Malaysian and Australian governments are frightened of being overrun by illegal immigrants and, as a result, corruption amongst the local officials is rife.

Background: Stephen Wallace's turgid, melodramatic movie veers between message movie and manipulative tear-jerker. Failing to address the very real problem of the Vietnamese boat people—an armada of escaping refugees that started as Vietnam fell under Communist rule—*Turtle Beach* is a forgettable little film with only Joan Chen's customarily excellent performance to recommend it. A far better cinematic treatment of the issue came out of Hong Kong in 1983's *The Boat People*. Art Malik and Greta Scacchi's soft-core love affair is preposterously handled and Malik has to cope with ridiculous lines like: "if they weren't so crushed by life they'd be more moderate in their enjoyment … don't be frightened, it's just the poor having fun." Malik's sole purpose seems to be as nothing more than exotic love interest, while Chen's role as a former prostitute is a flimsy excuse for baring her derrière and indulging in a little hanky-panky with her British husband. The boat people's plight is barely touched on and simply justifies the film's travelogue footage, sex scenes and Judith's tearful realization that motherhood is more important than her career—ah!

Heaven & Earth (1993)

Crew: Director: Oliver Stone. Producers: Oliver Stone, Arnon Milchan, Robert Kline, A Kitman Ho. Writer: Oliver Stone based on *When Heaven & Earth Changed Places* by Le Ly Hayslip and Jay Wurts and *Child Of War, Woman Of Peace* by Le Ly Hayslip and James Hayslip. Cinematographer: Robert Richardson. Editors: David Brenner, Sally Menke.

Cast: Tommy Lee Jones (Steve Butler), Joan Chen (Mama), Haing S Ngor (Papa), Hiep Thi Le (Le Ly).

Summary: Le Ly is a Vietnamese peasant whose family has lived through the Chinese, Japanese and French invasions. Growing up under the shadow of the VC, she finds herself caught up in "the American War" until she marries Steve Butler and travels to America with him. Life in the U.S. isn't as wonderful as she'd hoped and her new husband turns out to be violent and abusive. When she returns home to Vietnam with her American-Vietnamese children she discovers a country ravaged by the war and the years of political upheaval.

Subtext: Trading on a simplistic Buddhist subtext, *Heaven & Earth* treats life as a circular pattern of birth and death, something emphasized by the rice paddies, where grains of rice are grown, eaten and sown in a never-ending procession. Caught between heaven (Ong Troi) and Earth (Me Dat) are the people who must make their way through the inevitable struggles and joys of life.

Background: The only Hollywood film to give a Vietnamese perspective on the war, Oliver Stone's *Heaven & Earth* is portentous, overlong and completely unconvincing. Returning to the Vietnam War, Stone takes an apparently unusual approach to the conflict by ostensibly dumping the militaristic action of his earlier films in favour of a sympathetic portrayal of the Vietnamese experience of the war and its aftermath. Scoring top marks for his willingness to acknowledge the fact that 99.9% of Hollywood's Vietnam War films obscure the Vietnamese perspective, Stone then loses all these brownie points by turning the story into a flaccid tear-jerker. It's interesting that Hollywood has yet to make a film about a Vietnamese soldier's perspective—clearly this 'feminine' movie didn't offend anyone in the same way as a film about a VC fighter or North Vietnamese regular would have done.

Although the script self-consciously styles itself as both a family melodrama and a 'woman's' picture, Stone tries to inject some machismo into the proceedings, piling on the flashy visuals, sandwiching Hayslip's story between as many explosions as possible and generally playing this tender tale as though it's yet another of his macho polemics. For all his liberal posturing, Stone effectively tramples over Hayslip's autobiography with size twelve combat boots, following a film-making by numbers guide that's uncertain how to cope with anything other than Tommy Lee Jones' conventional post-traumatic stress breakdown. But not even the ever-dependable Tommy Lee can save this, if only because his blustering presence further undermines the film's heroine. What's more, the script's tacked-on Buddhist concerns with karma, spiritual development and redemption are embarrassingly facile. Hayslip deserved a much better treatment that this.

Cyclo (Xich Lo) (1995)

Crew: Director: Tran Anh Hung. Producer: Christophe Rossignon. Writer: Tran Anh Hung. Cinematographer: Benoît Delhomme. Editor: Nicole Dedieu.

Cast: Le Van Loc (Cyclo), Tran Nu Yen Khe (Sister), Tony Leung (Poet), Nguyen Nhu Quynh (Madam).

Summary: A young pedal cab cyclist is eking out a living on the streets of Ho Chi Minh City. His father is dead, his grandfather is frail and his sisters try their best to keep the money coming in. When his pedal cab is stolen by a rival gang, he's forced to turn to crime by gangster Poet (who has also lured his eldest sister into prostitution). Torn between honesty or starvation, Cyclo finds himself inexorably drawn into the underworld of the city.

Subtext: Tran Anh Hung's film focuses on the dangers that a lack of authority can bring. The film opens with Cyclo remembering the advice of his dead father about getting a "more dignified" job than a pedal cab driver. But what he is forced into is a life of crime that doesn't sit well with his father's advice. Without guidance, both he and his sister brutally lose their innocence.

Background: Although it's quite distinct from the director's previous feature, *The Scent Of Green Papaya* (which was set in the 1950s and focused on the story of a Vietnamese peasant's service in a French family's house), *Cyclo* is much like that earlier film in that it uses the seemingly non-political action to comment on the history of Vietnam. Although the 'American war' is never mentioned, its influence is felt throughout the film.

While *The Scent Of Green Papaya* focused on the years of French rule, *Cyclo* charts the post-1975 unification of the country under communist rule. The loss of innocence that the children suffer seems to have infected the whole of Ho Chi Minh City—the film's repeated images of purification (the constant use of water/washing) aren't enough to save the characters from their relentless slide into poverty and despair. The omnipresence of the American dollar in their misery is made quite clear in a series of close-ups of a dollar bill, the detailed shots of serial numbers and signatures emphasizing the fact that it is yankee dollars that

90

run Ho Chi Minh's criminal underworld and it is a mixture of greed for them and lack of them that keeps the system of exploitation (from prostitution to protection rackets) running. The need for transformation, symbolized by the film's use of paint and mud to make the film's two teenage boys unrecognisable, is paramount—but the only real agency of change that exists seems to be death.

8. Afterword

Is the Vietnam War film dead? Looking through the release dates for films about the conflict it's easy to see that the peak of our cinematic interest in that distant war has long since passed. The golden age of the cinema of Vietnam was in the 1970s. There were two, very different resurgences in the 1980s (one the *Rambo*-esque 'Return to 'Nam', the other the search for authenticity begun by Oliver Stone in *Platoon*). At the beginning of the 1990s there was yet another unexpected resurgence—though this time it wasn't combat films that were being made, but more thoughtful, reflective pieces like *Born On The Fourth Of July*, *Heaven & Earth* and *Dogfight*. Wearing their liberal anti-war temperament on their sleeves, these films looked like they might signal the last gasps of the Vietnam War genre. After all, the war was almost thirty years old.

But the turn of the millennium hasn't yet seen the end of the genre. Vietnam War films have high on the list of people's favourite movies (*The Deer Hunter*, *Apocalypse Now* and *Platoon* for instance) and have still exercised a big influence on popular culture—Vietnam vets continue to turn up in unlikely places, even cartoon shows like *South Park* and *King Of The Hill*. At the time of writing, at least two recent releases, *Tigerland* and *We Were Soldiers*, have signalled an unabashed return to the genre, the onslaught of DVD releases has kept films like *Full Metal Jacket* in the public eye and Francis Ford Coppola has confounded the brains and numbed the backsides of audiences who sat through his extended version of *Apocalypse Now Redux*. Vietnam, it seems, is a subject that America (and the rest of the world) is still willing to pay money to see on screen.

So maybe the Vietnam genre isn't ready to be dead and buried just yet. Writing this book in 2001, as military strikes continue against Afghanistan, Vietnam seems more relevant than ever. It's a watchword for America's over-commitment, for getting embroiled in a war that can't be won. In light of the military and foreign policy decisions being taken after September 11th, it seems that Vietnam still has a hold over America's psyche. Perhaps that's why the Vietnam War films remain such a powerful cultural force—it doesn't really matter that the bulk of the genre's texts have already been made, they continue to influence cinema and reflect on America's military choices. And that, from any perspective, is a sure sign that the genre's still alive and kicking.

9. Resource Materials

Books

Adair, Gilbert, *Hollywood's Vietnam: From The Green Berets To Full Metal Jacket* (London: William Heinemann, 1989).

Anderegg, Michael ed., *Inventing Vietnam: The War In Film And Television* (Philadelphia: Temple University Press, 1991).

Devine, Jeremy M, *Vietnam At 24 Frames A Second: A Critical And Thematic Analysis Of Over 400 Films About The Vietnam War* (Austin, Texas: University of Texas Press, 1995).

Dittmar, Linda and Gene Michaud, *From Hanoi To Hollywood: The Vietnam War In American Film* (New Brunswick: Rutgers UP, 1990).

Hellmann, John, *American Myth And The Legacy Of Vietnam* (New York: Columbia Press, 1986).

Herr, Michael, *Dispatches* (New York: Alfred Knopf, 1977).

Jeffords, Susan, *The Remasculinization Of America: Gender And The Vietnam War* (Bloomington, IN: Indiana University Press, 1989).

Klein, Michael ed., *The Vietnam Era: Media And Popular Culture In The US And Vietnam* (London: Pluto Press, 1990).

Kolko, Gabriel, *Anatomy Of A War: Vietnam, The United States and The Modern Historical Experience* (London: Allen and Unwin, 1986).

MacDonald, J Fred, *Television And The Red Menace: The Video Road To Vietnam* (New York: Praeger, 1985).

Malo, Jean-Jacques and Tony Williams eds., *Vietnam War Films: Over 600 Feature, Made-For-TV, Pilot and Short Movies, 1939-1994 From The United States, Vietnam, France, Belgium, Australia, Hong Kong, South Africa, Great Britain and Other Countries* (Jefferson, NC and London: McFarland and Co., 1994).

Mason, Robert, *Chicken Hawk* (London: Corgi Books, 1984).

Muse, Eben J, *The Vietnam War In American Film* (Lanham, MD: The Scarecrow Press, 1995).

Palmer, William J ed., *The Films Of The Seventies: A Social History* (Metuchen, NJ and London: Scarecrow Press, 1987).

Searle, William J ed, *Search And Clear: Critical Responses To Selected Literature And Films Of The Vietnam War* (Bowling Green, Ohio: Bowling Green State University Press, 1988).

Walker, Mark, *Vietnam Veteran Films* (Metuchen, NJ and London: Scarecrow Press, 1991).

Walsh, Jeffrey and James Aulich eds., *Vietnam Images: War And Representation* (Basingstoke, Hants: Macmillan, 1989).

Wilson, James C, *Vietnam In Prose And Film* (Jefferson, NC and London: MacFarland and Co., 1982).

Web Resources

Vietnam War Internet Project: www.vwip.org

Vietnam War History: www.vietnampix.com

Stanley Kubrick: www.kubrickfilms.warnerbros.com

Oliver Stone: www.oscarworld.net/ostone

Apocalypse Now: http://film.tierranet.com/films/a.now/

The Essential Library: Currently Available

Film Directors:

Woody Allen (Revised)	Tim Burton	Ang Lee
Jane Campion*	John Carpenter	Steve Soderbergh
Jackie Chan	Joel & Ethan Coen	Clint Eastwood
David Cronenberg	Terry Gilliam*	Michael Mann
Alfred Hitchcock	Krzysztof Kieslowski*	Roman Polanski
Stanley Kubrick	Sergio Leone	Oliver Stone
David Lynch	Brian De Palma*	
Sam Peckinpah*	Ridley Scott	
Orson Welles	Billy Wilder	
Steven Spielberg	Mike Hodges	

Film Genres:

Blaxploitation Films	Bollywood	French New Wave
Horror Films	Spaghetti Westerns	Vietnam War Movies
Vampire Films*	Heroic Bloodshed*	
Slasher Movies	Film Noir	

Film Subjects:

Laurel & Hardy	Marx Brothers	Animation
Steve McQueen*	Marilyn Monroe	The Oscars®
Filming On A Microbudget	Bruce Lee	Film Music

TV:

Doctor Who

Literature:

Cyberpunk	Philip K Dick	The Beat Generation
Agatha Christie	Sherlock Holmes	Noir Fiction*
Terry Pratchett	Hitchhiker's Guide	Alan Moore
Stephen King		

Ideas:

Conspiracy Theories	Nietzsche	UFOs
Feminism	Freud & Psychoanalysis	Bisexuality

History:

Alchemy & Alchemists	The Crusades	The Black Death
Jack The Ripper	The Rise Of New Labour	Ancient Greece
American Civil War	American Indian Wars	

Miscellaneous:

The Madchester Scene	Stock Market Essentials	Beastie Boys
How To Succeed As A Sports Agent		

Available at all good bookstores or send a cheque (payable to 'Oldcastle Books') to: **Pocket Essentials (Dept VWM), 18 Coleswood Rd, Harpenden, Herts, AL5 1EQ, UK.** £3.99 each (£2.99 if marked with an *) . For each book add 50p postage & packing in the UK and £1 elsewhere.